At Issue

Is Media Violence a Problem?

Other Books in the At Issue Series:

At Issue

Is Media Violence a Problem?

Stefan Kiesbye, Book Editor

GREENHAVEN PRESS
A part of Gale, Cengage Learning

GALE
CENGAGE Learning

Detroit • New York • San Francisco • New Haven, Conn • Waterville, Maine • London

Christine Nasso, *Publisher*
Elizabeth Des Chenes, *Managing Editor*

© 2010 Greenhaven Press, a part of Gale, Cengage Learning.

Gale and Greenhaven Press are registered trademarks used herein under license.

For more information, contact:
Greenhaven Press
27500 Drake Rd.
Farmington Hills, MI 48331-3535
Or you can visit our Internet site at gale.cengage.com

For product information and technology assistance, contact us at

Gale Customer Support, 1-800-877-4253
For permission to use material from this text or product, submit all requests online at www.cengage.com/permissions

Further permissions questions can be e-mailed to permissionrequest@cengage.com

Articles in Greenhaven Press anthologies are often edited for length to meet page requirements. In addition, original titles of these works are changed to clearly present the main thesis and to explicitly indicate the author's opinion. Every effort is made to ensure that Greenhaven Press accurately reflects the original intent of the authors. Every effort has been made to trace the owners of copyrighted material.

Cover photograph reproduced by permission of Brand X Pictures.

LIBRARY OF CONGRESS CATALOGING-IN-PUBLICATION DATA

Is media violence a problem? / Stefan Kiesbye, book editor.
        p. cm. -- (At issue)
    Includes bibliographical references and index.
    ISBN 978-0-7377-4886-4 (hardcover) -- ISBN 978-0-7377-4887-1 (pbk.)
    1. Violence in mass media. 2. Mass media--Social aspects. I. Kiesbye, Stefan.
    P96.V5I82 2010
    303.6--dc22

                                                    2010005726

Printed in the United States of America
 2 3 4 5 6   19 18 17 16 15

Contents

Introduction

Most perpetrators of vicious crimes don't blame the media or claim to have imitated a violent television show, such as Showtime's *Dexter*, nor do they assert that crime shows provided them with a blueprint for their actions. Most adults, it is said, can make a clear distinction between reality and make-believe. They understand the repercussions of their actions and are held responsible. When it comes to children, however, it is less apparent what they know and understand about violent images they see. On June 26, 2002, Charnicia Huggins, a reporter for Reuters, wrote about a five-year-old boy who nearly killed his twenty-two-month-old cousin when he acted out a wrestling move he had just seen on TV. She writes, "The five-year-old child performed a 'pile-driver' move in which he placed his cousin's head between both of his knees, lifted the infant's body and dropped to the ground." The infant's head hit the ground, and the child was later diagnosed with a spinal cord injury.

Television and movie violence has existed for many decades, and even before shooting games entered the market, people were aware of the influence violent stories can have on the minds of young children. In its June 1982 issue, *Playboy* interviewed Brandon Tartikoff, then president of NBC, and he recounted an episode from his own childhood:

> Television did have an effect on me right from the beginning. In first grade, I was a member of a four-kid gang that went around imitating TV Westerns. We'd disrupt class to play out scenes, picking up chairs and hitting people over the head with them—except, unlike on TV, the chairs didn't break, the kids did. Finally, the teacher called my parents in and said, "Obviously, he's being influenced by these TV shows, and if he's to continue in this class, you've got to agree not to let him watch television anymore." So, from

first to second grade there was a dark period during which I didn't watch TV at all. And I calmed down and the gang broke up.

While critics of media violence point to numerous examples that suggest a direct causal link between media and real-life violence, the picture emerging from decades of research is far from simple. For every instance in which a kid acted out violent scenes from a movie or TV show, there are thousands of others in which watching violence did no apparent harm. And despite the notoriety of violent episodes, they are relatively scarce. Many researchers are more concerned about the long-term effects of being surrounded by violent media.

For example, with the growing sophistication of video game graphics, which put players in near lifelike situations, some researchers wonder whether gamers have also become more sophisticated in their differentiation between story and life, or whether they are entering a shadow world in which distinctions between what can be rebooted and what is irreversible are blurred beyond recognition.

Complicating the issue are claims made by Lt. Col. (Ret.) Dave Grossman, a former U.S. Army Ranger and tactical trainer, in a 2006 article by Mark and Keisha Hoerrner in *Children's Voice*. Grossman contends that shooting games train kids for real-life violence. He cites a 1997 high school shooting in Paducah, Kentucky, as evidence. A teenage boy fired on a group of peers and hit five people in the head, a difficult feat even for trained law enforcement officers. The boy had spent many hours playing first-person shooter games, but had never practiced with a real gun before.

In an interesting turn of events, the Army has begun to use the appeal of shooting games for recruitment purposes. *America's Army* has been a huge success, finds Michael Reagan in a July 23, 2008, article for Truthout.com. He writes, "Most troubling of all, these recruitment and training techniques are targeted at children. Apart from sanitizing the violence of war, the Army toned down the gore in the game to get a Teen rating. . . ." Reagan adds, "Four years after the game was introduced at the 2002 Los Angeles E3 (Electronic Entertainment Expo), and halfway around the world in Mosul, Iraq, *America's Army* was having an effect. Sgt. Sinque Swales had just fired his .50-caliber machine gun at so called insurgents for only the second time. 'It felt like I was in a big video game,' he said. 'It didn't even faze me, shooting back. It was just natural instinct. Boom! Boom! Boom! Boom!'"

Yet video games, for all the negative publicity, might also help players develop skills that can be applied in real life. Sophisticated simulator games have been cited as useful tools to prepare soldiers for difficult battle situations. And, as explained by the Hoerrners, young players can derive similar benefits: "[Media violence researcher Craig A. Anderson] bought his son a copy of the flight simulator game *Flight Unlimited* and a realistic joystick and foot pedal. His son spent considerable time learning to fly, which paid off when the child went to a NASA summer camp and was assigned the role of pilot on a space shuttle mission simulator."

The debate over whether the harm media violence might cause outweighs the potential good will no doubt continue. So will the demand for violent movies and video games. *At Issue: Is Media Violence a Problem?* not only looks at the possible connection between media violence and aggression in children and adults, but also examines the society in which these media flourish. Guns are an integral part of American life, and the right to carry arms—school and mall shootings notwithstanding—has not been seriously challenged. When innocent bystanders die in a vicious attack, people scramble to find a cause and prevent a tragedy from happening again. Media violence all too often tops that list of causes, and calls for censorship—voluntary or forced—become louder. Concerned citizens and policy makers will continue to struggle with the question of whether violent movies and shooting games are the cause of violence in society or merely a reflection of the world around us.

1

Media Violence Causes Aggression in Children

Gina Simmons

Gina Simmons is codirector of Schneider Family Services and is a licensed marriage and family therapist. She developed the Manage Anger Daily for Teens program, which teaches teenagers how to express their anger in appropriate ways. Simmons is a former columnist for Living Better *magazine, and she publishes the M.A.D. TIMES, a quarterly newsletter with information about anger and stress management.*

American children spend an alarming and still increasing amount of time in front of screen media such as television, movies, and video games, and much of the content is of a violent nature, causing real-life aggression and violence. While scientists have long maintained that media violence is to blame for many acts of brutality in our society, they have not always communicated that view effectively and are outnumbered or silenced by those who stand to gain financially from the production and sale of movies and video games.

A national study in 1999 reported that the average American child spends about 40 hours per week viewing media (television, movies, video games, etc). Think about the lost potential of children spending the equivalent of a full-time job, passively viewing entertainment. No wonder childhood obesity is considered the fastest growing health problem in

Gina Simmons, "Does Violent Media Cause Aggression?" Schneider Family Services, September 30, 2008. www.manageangerdaily.com. Reproduced by permission of the publisher and the author.

America today. Alarmingly, American children consume a toxic dose of media violence. By the time the average American child completes elementary school he or she has seen 8,000 murders and over 100,000 other acts of violence on television. These figures are even higher if the child watches cable television or has a DVD or videocassette player.

The Link Between Media Violence and Real Violence

Many researchers have tried to determine why the rate of violent crime in the United States is so high compared with the rate of violence in other industrialized nations. They discovered a link between media violence and real violence. Historically, violence in the United States increased dramatically in 1965, when the first generation of television watchers became old enough to start committing violent crime. Studies in several countries show a similar pattern. As television is introduced into a new country, the rate of violent crime increases.

Historically, violence in the United States increased dramatically in 1965, when the first generation of television watchers became old enough to start committing violent crime.

An argument in support of violent media claims that just because there is a link, does not mean that violent media causes violence in the real world. However, in July 2000, six major professional associations signed a joint statement reporting, "At this time, well over 1,000 studies point overwhelmingly to a causal connection between media violence and aggressive behavior in some children." (American Psychological Association, the American Academy of Pediatrics, the American Academy of Child & Adolescent Psychiatry, the American Medical Association, the American Academy of Family Physicians, and the American Psychiatric Association).

The Case Against Media Violence

If the evidence linking violent media with violence in the real world is so strong, why isn't it being reported in the news media? A recent *Newsweek* magazine article even claimed that there was no reliable evidence showing that viewing violent media caused aggression. Scientists were told that *Newsweek* would not publish their rebuttal. The *New York Times* also refused to print a scientific rebuttal to an op-ed piece criticizing media violence research. [Brad J.] Bushman and [Craig A.] Anderson from Iowa State University have outlined a few reasons why the news media have failed to accurately report on the dangers of media violence:

1. Multinational, multimedia corporations have a huge financial interest in promoting the consumption of violent media around the world, and in suppressing evidence that would discourage people from consuming violent media.

2. Newspapers get a lot of their advertising revenue from the makers of violent media who advertise films and television programs.

3. Print news media may not wish to print controversial stories potentially offensive to their readers, thus losing subscriptions or advertisers.

4. Scientists are not good media spokespersons. They do not produce quick, dramatic sound bites on the 6 o'clock news. Scientists are trained to convey the limitations of their research, to speak in qualified, measured, moderate tones. This style of communicating can appear unconvincing and boring to the average consumer of media. Also, scientists do not typically have the time and money to lobby and promote their findings.

5. Journalists, in their desire to appear objective and fair, may promote contrary views, even those lacking scien-

tific scrutiny, in a misguided attempt to present more than one side of a controversial issue.

6. Those with a financial motivation to suppress information that discourages the consumption of violent media have a lot of money available to hire writers, attorneys, and others to confuse and mislead the public.

Reducing Children's Exposure to Media Violence

What can the average person do about this serious problem? First, get an education about the strong link between violent media and aggression. The American Psychological Association Web site is a good place to start. Second, limit the content and the time both you and your children consume media. One way to limit this is to set a family rule that for every hour of television watching or video games, you have to do one hour of exercise or outdoor activity. Third, encourage your children to engage in confidence-building activities such as athletics, art, music, dance, and science, instead of passively viewing entertainment. Fourth, share this information with family and friends. Finally, support legislation that allows consumers access to information about the content of the media, allowing parents to monitor and control what their children watch. We can reduce violence, one child at a time.

2

Media Violence Does Not Cause Aggressive Behavior in Children

Jonathan L. Freedman

Jonathan L. Freedman is a professor of psychology at the University of Toronto. He is the author of the book Media Violence and Its Effect on Aggression: Assessing the Scientific Evidence.

Despite a report from the Federal Communications Commission (FCC) on the causal link between media violence and aggressive human behavior, there is no scientific evidence that viewing violence on television makes people commit acts of violence in the real world. Most studies undertaken by scientists over the years have been biased or faulty and have taken sides without delivering proof for their various conclusions. If television and other media were to blame for an increased level of violence, crime rates would still be on the rise. Rates have declined, however, since peaking in the 1980s and early 1990s, despite ever more explicitly violent television shows, movies, and video games.

The recent release of the Federal Communications Commission (FCC) report on violent television programming and its call for restricting children's access to such programming has once more brought this issue to public attention. There have been many statements about this issue by psychologists, politicians, and others.

By those who believe that television violence is harmful, we have been told that there is overwhelming evidence that exposure to violence on television causes aggression (what I will call the causal hypothesis for convenience), that there is no longer any legitimate debate about this, and that the effect is as strong as the effect of cigarette smoking on cancer. We have even been told that the press is biased because it gives more time to the opposing view than is warranted—that since there is no question, the press should not even mention the other view.

A Lack of Evidence

None of this is correct. The evidence is not overwhelming—indeed, it provides no good reason to believe that television violence causes aggression, much less serious violence. The debate is certainly not over, although some would like it to be. There is no comparison between the effect of smoking on cancer and the effect of television violence on aggression. And the press has, if anything, given far too much attention to the causal hypothesis than to those who disagree with it. The most ardent advocates of the causal hypothesis seem to object to any disagreement or criticism of their position. However, their position is wrong, it deserves to be criticized, and it is time once more to set the record straight

It should be clear from the government reports on this issue that the evidence is not overwhelming and that the debate is not over. In the short time that we have been in the 21st century, the government has produced three reports dealing with the effect of media violence. The surgeon general's report on youth violence [*Youth Violence: A Report of the Surgeon General*] concluded that exposure to television violence causes a short-term increase in aggression, but went on to say that television violence has little or no role in causing real violence. The Federal Trade Commission (FTC) report concluded that exposure to media violence is correlated with aggression, but that the evidence is insufficient to know whether exposure to media violence *causes* the increase in aggression. The third report was released by the FCC on April 25, 2007.

The FCC Report on Television Violence

The statement in the FCC report is somewhat harder to understand, since it says: "We agree with the views of the surgeon general and find that, on balance, research provides strong evidence that exposure to violence in the media can increase aggressive behavior in children, at least in the short term." How can one say that on balance (implying that the conclusion is far from clear-cut) there is strong evidence? If there really is strong evidence, then it's not a question of "on balance." One cannot have both "on balance" and "strong evidence" in the same sentence and have it make sense. Despite this somewhat odd wording in the FCC report, none of these reports considered the evidence overwhelming and none of them declared the debate over.

There is no comparison between the effect of smoking on cancer and the effect of television violence on aggression.

It is unfortunate that the FCC report does not explain how it reached its conclusion. The early part of the report mentions opinions that disagree with the idea that television violence causes aggression. It also describes some criticisms on both sides of the dispute—arguments against the causal hypothesis and against those who disagree with that hypothesis. Fair enough! Listening to these kinds of arguments and taking them seriously is one way for a commission to decide which side to favor. But if one is going to say that the causal hypothesis is right (as the FCC does at least for short-term effects), there is some obligation to justify that decision. What convinced them? What are the key weaknesses of the criticisms of the research that supposedly supports the causal hypothesis? What are the key studies or arguments in favor of the hypothesis?

It is not enough to say that "on balance" the commission has decided that exposure to television violence causes aggression in the short run. As mild and moderate as that conclusion is, it is still a decision to pick one side of the debate over another. Judges in court have to give reasons for their decisions. That is the least we should expect from a multiyear study by the FCC. We did not get it.

A Missed Chance

This was a missed chance. The FCC could have paid serious attention to the actual evidence. It did not. Rather than analyzing the conflicting evidence and opinion, the report simply comes down on the side of those who believe that television violence is harmful. There is no careful analysis of the research, there is no careful explanation of their conclusions; there seems to be mainly an acceptance of that view because more of those they talked with favored it than favored the other view.

This is not the way science should work. It is not a popularity contest or a matter of consensus. It is or should be the research findings that matter, but alas, the FCC review does not seem to have spent the substantial time that would have been necessary actually to read the original research. Too bad. A careful, analytic review of all of the research by people with no preconceptions would have been valuable. A cursory sampling of scientific opinion and a fair amount of nonscientific opinion could not hope to provide anything of much use. . . .

Science vs. Opinion

Let me start by distinguishing science from opinion. The FCC notes that several organizations that represent health care professionals and scientists have declared that television violence is harmful. If these organizations had undertaken careful reviews of the research, their statements might be given some weight because they would be based on scientific research.

However, it is obvious that the statements are not based on any such reviews. This is clear from the fact that the statements contain serious errors of fact.

For example, the American Academy of Pediatrics (AAP) issued a statement in 2001 stating that exposure to television violence was harmful and urging parents to restrict children's access to television violence and, indeed, to avoid any television exposure for children under 2 years of age. In making the statement that television violence was harmful, the AAP referred to more than 3,500 research studies with all but 18 showing a positive relationship (between exposure to violence and aggression). This is wildly inaccurate. As anyone familiar with the literature knows, there are about 250 studies on this topic and there are certainly many more than 18 that failed to find an effect.

This is not the way science should work. . . . It is or should be the research findings that matter.

The FCC report quotes Craig [A.] Anderson, who excuses these errors by saying they were due merely to confusion about what to count—that the AAP was counting all articles on the subject, not just independent research studies. While Anderson may be forgiven for defending every statement in favor of his position, his explanation makes no sense. In the first place, the statement clearly says "research studies." Moreover, the reference to the 18 that failed to get an effect cannot possibly be to all articles but must be to research. And note that the reference to the failed studies is not a round number. It does not say "about 20" or "about 30"—it says "18," which is a precise number. One should be able to assume that they have the list of those 18 negative studies and could readily produce it.

Misleading Statements

But the AAP does not have such a list, because there is no such list. Their statement is obviously made without any detailed knowledge of the research. Other organizations, including the American Psychological Association, which surely should know better, have made similar though not quite as spectacular errors when referring to the number of studies. Therefore, we must assume that these statements are based not on science but on some combination of listening to what others tell these organizations, their own intuition, political expediency, and, I hope, real concern for our children. Since the statements are not based on science, they should be ignored. Yet the FCC report mentions that these organizations have supported the causal hypothesis and seems to give that some weight.

Everyone is entitled to an opinion on this or any other topic, but these opinions have no scientific standing. All that matters is what the research shows. There can be disagreements about how to interpret research findings, how much weight to give to particular studies, and so on. Nevertheless, in the end, informed decisions have to be based on the research and conclusions have to be justified in terms of the actual research findings.

Research Findings

Correlation. First, most of the relevant work has shown that there is a correlation between exposure to violent television programming and aggression. That is, children who are exposed to more television violence tend to be more aggressive, and vice versa. The relationship is weak, but fairly consistent. However, as the FTC pointed out, the existence of this relationship does not indicate any causal relationship. It provides no evidence that exposure to television violence *causes* children to be aggressive. The most likely explanation of the relationship is that some children are more aggressive in general than others, and that the more aggressive children prefer violent television, watch and play more aggressive games, and act more aggressively themselves. To demonstrate that violent television *causes* aggressiveness, it is necessary to rule out this simple, intuitive explanation that is almost certainly at least partially true.

Experimental research. This is the only type of research that can provide clear evidence about causality. The great majority of studies on the effect of exposure to television violence have been experimental. In the typical experiment, some children are shown a program containing violence and others are shown a nonviolent program. The children are then given an opportunity to act aggressively. If those who have seen the violent program act more aggressively than the others, this supports the hypothesis that violent television causes aggression. . . .

Everyone is entitled to an opinion on this or any other topic, but these opinions have no scientific standing.

There are many problems with much of this research. . . . Although those who favor the causal hypothesis persist in describing these findings as overwhelmingly supportive of their position, that is not correct. In fact, the majority of the studies do not provide such support. . . .

With and Without Television

Several studies have looked at what happens when television is introduced into a country or a community. If television causes aggression and violent behavior, assuming that the television programming contains some violence, there should be more and more violent crime after television is available. [Brandon] Centerwall compared the United States and Canada after the introduction of television with South Africa, which during the same period did not have television. The argument was that because the crime rate went up in the United States and Canada but not in South Africa, this showed that television caused crime.

As many have pointed out, this makes little sense since one cannot compare the situation in the three countries. In addition, other countries that also got television at the same time as the United States and Canada did not have the same increase in crime. I think this study has been thoroughly discredited and I was surprised to see the FCC refer to it (although the report did include some of the criticisms).

Another study identified three small communities in Canada. One of these had several television stations, one had only one station, and the third had no television. It was known that television was about to be introduced into the third community, so the researchers obtained measures of aggression in all three communities before and after the third community got television. The authors report that aggression went up in the third community compared to the others.

Not one method has produced a clear majority of findings consistent with the idea that exposure to violent television makes people aggressive.

Mistake-Prone Research

As with the comparison of countries, this study suffers from the insurmountable problem that the three communities differ in many ways that could explain the finding. Moreover, the actual results were far weaker than reported, failed to distinguish between real and play aggression, and were not consistent across measures. In any case, the television that was introduced into the third community was from the Canadian Broadcasting Company [CBC] and had virtually no programs that contained any amount of violence. Thus, even if it could be shown that there was an effect, it could not have been due to violent programming.

A far better study looked at several hundred U.S. cities during a period when television licenses were temporarily frozen and then unfrozen three years later. The argument was that if television caused crime, there should be a relative increase in crime in those cities with television compared to those without, and that the difference should disappear once all cities had television. The findings provide no support for the causal hypothesis. There was no change in violent crimes, car theft, or burglary during the key period. Oddly, there was more larceny in communities with television than in the have-not communities. This difference disappeared when they all had television. The authors attribute this to feelings of envy because television showed mostly middle- or upper-class households. Whatever the explanation of this effect, it is clear that the study does not support the notion that television violence causes aggression or violent behavior....

Research Is Inconclusive

Those who favor the causal hypothesis often say that although one type of research may not be conclusive, there is a confluence of findings such that all of the methods produce support. The opposite is true. That is, there is a confluence of findings such that all of the methods *fail* to produce support for the causal hypothesis. Not one method has produced a clear majority of findings consistent with the idea that exposure to violent television makes people aggressive. It is not true for children and it is not true for adults.

Far from the overwhelming evidence that those who favor the hypothesis promote, the evidence overall and from each type of study is inconsistent, weak, and generally nonsupportive.... A thorough reading of all of the research indicates that either there is no effect of violent television on aggression or, if there is any effect, it is vanishingly small. . . .

Comparing Violence to Smoking and Cancer

One of the most deceptive statements coming from those who favor the causal hypothesis is that the effect of television violence on aggression is as strong as the effect of smoking on lung cancer. This is hyperbole of the most egregious kind because it is not only wrong but might cause people to question the harmful effects of smoking. I am not an expert on the effects of smoking, but let me cite one figure: Someone who smokes regularly for 20 years is 10 to 20 times more likely to get lung cancer than someone who does not smoke.

There is nothing remotely comparable in any of the research on television violence. It is not true that someone who watches television violence for any length of time, no matter how long, is many times more likely to commit a violent crime than someone who does not watch. In fact, there is no reliable evidence that television violence causes any violent crimes. And even with minor aggression, there is no evidence that watching violent television causes people to be many times more likely to be aggressive. It does not even make sense to talk about it in those terms.

In addition, the relationship between smoking and cancer shows all of the effects that would be expected if smoking causes cancer. The more cigarettes people smoke, the more likely they are to get cancer; the more years they smoke, the more likely they are to get cancer; if they stop smoking, their risk of cancer decreases. In contrast, there is no evidence that the more years people are exposed to violent television, the more aggressive they are; or that if they stop watching violent television, they become less aggressive. These so called dose-response effects are crucial for the scientific case to be made, and they simply do not exist.

Having raised the issue of smoking and cancer, let me use it to contrast what the real world tells us about that and about television violence and aggression. If smoking causes lung cancer, there should be observable effects on real people living in the real world. It is not enough to show that smokers are more likely to get lung cancer, because there might conceivably be other explanations for that. However, we can make more precise predictions.

About 10 years after television was introduced into the United States, the rate of violent crime began to go up and increased dramatically from 1965 to 1980.

In the early part of the 20th century, most women in the United States did not smoke because it was not considered proper. We should therefore expect that during that period, the rate of lung cancer in men should have been much higher than in women. It was! Later in the century, attitudes changed and women began to smoke. We should expect that the rates of lung cancer in women would begin to go up and eventually become close to those in men. They did! In other words, what occurred in the real world was just what we would expect if smoking caused lung cancer. This is not definitive proof of the effect, but if we had not seen this relationship, it sure would have made us wonder and perhaps question our assumption about smoking and cancer.

How about television violence? If it causes people to be more aggressive, we should expect that to show up in rates of violent crime. About 10 years after television was introduced into the United States, the rate of violent crime began to go up and increased dramatically from 1965 to 1980. One possible explanation was that the increase was caused by exposure to television violence. The explanation of the time lag for the increase was that the effect would be mainly on children, and that it would take several years until they got old enough to begin committing violent crimes. So when the crime rate began to increase, many people blamed it on television. Of course, many other factors could have caused the increase, but television was a convenient (though I would say implausible) target.

However, it is incumbent on those blaming television to follow through on their analysis. After about 1980 the rate of violent crime leveled off in the United States until about 1992. At that point, we still had lots of violent programming on television, we had vivid and more and more realistic violence in films, we had violent lyrics in rap music, and we had the rapidly growing popularity of video games, especially violent video games being played by young males. If violent television causes aggression, and if (as many of the same people believe) violent movies, violent lyrics in rap music, and violent video games cause aggression, the rate of violent crime should have gone through the roof.

That did not happen. Instead, there was a sharp decline in violent crime that started in 1992 and continued to the point that the rate is now below what it was before television became popular. And just to be clear, this was not due to a change in demographics, since the drop in violent crime rate was particularly sharp among young males who are the ones who commit a disproportionate number of such crimes.

The Case Against the Causal Hypothesis

This by itself, though clearly inconsistent with the causal hypothesis, does not disprove it. Many other explanations of the pattern are possible. But surely it must make those who favor the hypothesis, and who blamed television for the earlier increase, wonder why we did not see the pattern they should have predicted. It should also give pause to those legislators who are concerned about the harmful effects of television violence. They should ask themselves why, if television is so harmful, there is less violent crime now than there was when they were young.

The FCC's conclusion that exposure to television violence makes children aggressive is not justified by the scientific evidence. Despite many statements to the contrary, the research does not support the hypothesis that television violence causes aggression. The findings from every methodological approach are mostly not supportive. There is no confluence of support from the various approaches, but exactly the opposite—a confluence of nonsupport from the various approaches. Moreover, the dramatic decline in violent crime that has occurred since 1992 contradicts the notion that exposure to violent media of all kinds causes people to behave violently.

In sum, there is no convincing scientific evidence that television violence causes children to be aggressive, or that any particular depiction of violence on television has this effect, or that it affects any particular type of children more than others. There has been a considerable amount of research on this topic—enough so that if there were an effect, the research should have shown it. Therefore, my conclusion is that either there is no effect of television violence on aggression, or, if there is an effect, it is vanishingly small because otherwise the research would have found it.

3

Viewers' Responses to Violent Media Are Complex and Varied

David Trend

David Trend is professor of studio art at the University of California, Irvine. He is editor of the book Reading Digital Culture.

Researchers trying to find a causal relationship between media violence and aggressive behavior of audiences underestimate the complexity of the viewing process. Television or movie audiences understand violent images on many levels. Depending on the sophistication of the viewers or the context in which they watch violence, a film can elicit very different responses from different viewers. While many studies decry the lifelike representation of violence in recent movies, the images have been highly and artificially altered to serve a filmmaker's vision and to comment ironically and even critically on violence. Less sophisticated audiences, however, might not understand a filmmaker's intention and may get the general perception that the world is a violent place in which violence is the best way to solve problems.

Social scientists conducting media violence research can be uninformed about perspectives from media studies—and they consequently approach media violence with a disciplinary bias. Social science "effects" researchers often apply what might be termed a "correspondence" or "transmission" theory of communication that sees information moving unilaterally and unproblematically from image to viewer. People who study media know this is incorrect. Informed by theories of language and reception, media studies recognizes that a movie can convey many kinds of messages simultaneously that will be understood differently by different viewers. How one perceives a piece of media is affected by the knowledge, experience, and background one brings to the encounter, as well as the viewing context. Moreover, audiences do not simply take in what they are shown. Instead they engage in an ongoing exchange with the movie in which they develop expectations about what will happen next. In the process viewers may accept, reject, or ignore parts of the message—or they may invent meanings quite different than those intended by the maker. Meaning is always a matter of negotiation. This is why efforts to pin down correlations between media violence and aggression have been so difficult.

The Pleasure of Terror

Also, media violence is extremely difficult to define and quantify. Is it simply a matter of depicting physical harm? Does it need to be aggressive or intentional? What about accidents or natural disasters? Does psychological torment count? What about verbal or implied violence? Are there degrees of violence? Is justified violence better for viewers than the gratuitous variety? What about humorous violence? Sports? The answer is that no one really knows. As [W.] James Potter wrote in his landmark overview of the effects field, *On Media Violence*, "In the literature on media violence, definitions of violence vary widely. There is no consensus. . . . These conditions make it very difficult to synthesize findings across studies." The NTVS [National Television Violence Study] grappled with this problem in asserting differential effects from different forms of media violence. Potter was one of the senior investigators of the NTVS, which stated in its summary report:

The same research that shows that televised violence can have harmful effects also demonstrates that not all violence portrayals are problematic. There are many ways to depict violence. For example, the violence may occur on screen and be shown graphically, or it may occur offscreen but be clearly implied. Violent acts may be shown close up or at a distance. There are also differences in the types of characters who commit violence and their reasons for doing so. And there are differences in the outcomes of violence—some depictions focus on the pain and suffering of victims, whereas others avoid showing the negative consequences of physical aggression. Simply put, not all portrayals of violence are the same. Their context can vary in many important ways. Studies show that the way in which violence is presented helps to determine whether portrayal might be harmful to viewers.

Violent Media Work on Many Levels

Beyond the issue of whether or not media violence causes harm is the more provocative question of why people choose to watch. What desires does media violence satisfy? What pleasures, if any, does it provide? How does media violence work?

How one perceives a piece of media is affected by the knowledge, experience, and background one brings to the encounter, as well as the viewing context.

Part of the answer is media-specific. Movies, television, computer games, and print media structure information differently. In a movie theater, viewers are more easily drawn into the viewing space of the screen that enables the suspension of disbelief in the artifice of the film. Distraction is minimized spatially by a darkened theater and temporally by the absence of commercial interruptions, as well as the social convention of remaining seated throughout the movie. In contrast, television must fight for attention, functioning as a source of entertainment, news, and background noise. Rather than delivering discrete narratives, network television offers a jumble of program segments, commercials, and new updates that viewers experience in what Raymond Williams termed a "flow." Satellite, cable, and recording technologies enable programs to be manipulated, repeated, and rescheduled. Computer games and the Internet introduce the element of inter-activity.

Tweaking "Reality"

The assertion is often made that violence in the media is becoming increasingly graphic and "real." In fact the opposite is taking place. Part of what makes media violence appealing to viewers is the extent to which it is anesthetized and transformed by production technologies. Director Sam Peckinpah is regarded as one of the pioneers in such work, beginning with his film *The Wild Bunch*. In that film, gunfights were depicted using shots from numerous cameras to create a sense of spatial movement and depth. Rapidly changing footage displayed at normal speed was intercut with slow-motion imagery that drew in viewers at key moments. More recently, Steven Spielberg's *Saving Private Ryan* (1998)—a film that many war veterans say captured the genuine "feel" of battle—relied on a veritable smorgasbord of techniques and tricks to generate the sensation of verisimilitude. Manipulations of camera shutter speeds created a jerky "pixilated" experience of action scenes, as did the intentional interference with camera sync. Use of an "image shaker" gave the impression of nearby explosions. Exaggerations of handheld camera movements—typically corrected by flexicam technology—gave some scenes the "realistic" sense of documentary footage shot on the run. Tampering with the coating of lenses gave some scenes an eerie atmospheric look. Chemical treatments to the film increased the contrast and density of shadows. As Stephen Prince observed, "These techniques gave the violence an elaborate and explicit aesthetic frame, which was intensified by the picture's narrative of heroism and moral redemption. The violence was not raw, that is, it was not real. It was staged for the camera and filtered through various effects and technologies."

This aestheticization of violence makes it tolerable and enjoyable. Through the pyrotechnics of cinematic technology and special effects, portrayals of such "cartoon violence" become bombastic spectacles of excess. The entertainment industry is well aware of how this process works. As the technology of computer-generated special effects has improved in the past decade, its costs have fallen dramatically. This is another reason for the proliferation of violent spectacles. Besides appealing to the broadest domestic audience demographics and besides their international marketability in non-English-speaking "after-markets," movies heavy with digital special effects are cheap to make. This financial incentive not only drives the selection of films a production company will make, it increasingly is a factor in how movies initially are conceived. Movie violence has become the central idea upon which many films are based.

The assertion is often made that violence in the media is becoming increasingly graphic and "real." In fact the opposite is taking place.

The "New Violence"

More than one critic has commented that violence has become such a driving force in many action films that spectacular moments like long car chases, nuclear bomb explosions, earthquakes, and photon beam blasts have achieved more prominence than character, plot, or story line. In fact, one of the funnier aspects of studying contemporary action films is that the occurrence of extraordinary pyrotechnics often makes no sense whatsoever. This is certainly true in such action thrillers as *Crank* (2006), *Miami Vice* (2006), and *The Fast and the Furious: Tokyo Drift* (2006). The nonsensical character of movie violence has become so extreme that it has inspired a new subgenre of films—termed the "new violence" movies— that mimic or poke fun at action movies. Oliver Stone's *Natural Born Killers* (1994) [and] Quentin Tarantino's *Kill Bill: [Vol.] 1* (2003), *Kill Bill: [Vol.] 2* (2004), and *Grindhouse* (2006) all use violence to such excess that they make critical comments on the genre. New-violence films have also been produced by the growing movie industries in Japan, India, and other Asian nations. The hit Japanese cult movies *Battle Royale* (2000), *Suicide Club* (2000), *Ichi the Killer* (2002), and *The Grudge* (2004) all use excessive violence with a sense of critique and have been rewarded at prestigious film festivals for the intelligent ways they examine violence in relationship to other social issues. The one problem with such postmodern copying or appropriation of older styles of violence is that audiences often don't grasp the irony or the joke. Many viewers walked out of films like *Natural Born Killers* and *Kill Bill* with the conviction that moviemaking has reached an all-time low and that impressionable viewers will probably imitate the violence the films depict. Indeed, many viewers are drawn to these new-violence movies exactly for the excitement that they derive from taking in the cartoonish violence the films provide. What is the real downside of the new-violence movies, if any? The answer is that few viewers will be moved to emulate the killers they see on the screen, but they may take away from the movies something even more problematic: an enhanced belief that the world is a violent place, that violence is a good way to solve problems, and that violent characters are people to be admired and emulated.

4

Movies Don't Facilitate Violence—Gun Laws Do

James Rocchi

Film critic James Rocchi writes for MSN Movies and the Now or Then column for the American Movie Classics Web site. He's written about pop culture and movies for publications such as Mother Jones *and* Metro Newspapers, *and he was the film critic for Netflix from 2001 to 2005 and the film critic for San Francisco's CBS 5 from 2005 to 2008.*

After each of the recent school shootings, commentators and politicians have called for stricter laws governing television content and video games, citing the bad influence violent media had on the shooters. Yet no evidence exists to sustain such arguments, and the discussion about media violence is a smoke screen, keeping U.S. society from having a discussion about the real culprit: guns. In all school shootings, minors or mentally unstable adults were able to buy guns, often legally and without an appropriate background check. They were able to buy ammunition and fulfill their violent fantasies, acts that stricter gun laws could have prevented.

I had already been thinking about violence in entertainment since I saw *Funny Games* at Sundance [film festival]; Michael Haneke's English-language remake of his own 1997 film is a grim piece of moviemaking, and one designed to start arguments about why and how we watch violent films. And then the NIU [Northern Illinois University] school shooting last

James Rocchi, "The Moviegoer: School Shootings, Violent Entertainment and Other Funny Games," *Huffington Post*, February 19, 2008. Reproduced by permission.

Thursday [February 2008] brought all those thoughts to the front of my brain, with Illinois legislator Rep. Robert Pritchard imploring us to examine a "culture of violence" in movies and video games, and FOX News guest and headline-grabbing hack Jack Thompson suggesting that violent video games played a role in events at NIU. Anytime there's a mass shooting, it seems, the discussion comes up as to whether or not violent culture leads to violent acts.

Cultural conservatives on the Right and Left, though, can't explain why the gun-toting action of some anime and films like Battle Royale *isn't being recreated in the streets of Tokyo on a regular basis.*

Responding to Continued Criticism

As a film critic, I can only say one thing in response to those cultural pundits on the Right and Left who suggest that mass shootings are inspired by movies and video games, which is, simply, "You're wrong." And that may seem a little sharp, but now and then a little sharpness is the only way to even scratch the stone-solid wrongheadedness of some people's thought processes. There are a variety of exercises in logic one can run though to demolish the theory that violent entertainment correlates to violent activity in a matter of seconds. Various mechanisms distribute American pop culture throughout the world, whether legal ones like multinational theatrical and DVD distribution or illegal ones like DVD piracy and peer-to-peer downloading. American pop culture is viewed and appreciated (or, in some cases, viewed and despised) worldwide by a large, avid audience. And yet, Western democracies like Germany, Canada, Australia and Britain don't have a statistically similar rate of mass shootings or gun murders. Economically and demographically similar audiences are watching these films, and yet, viewers in other nations aren't making the leap to arming themselves and shooting people as the final possible act of film appreciation.

And, as I've joked with gallows humor before when this line of argument comes up, if you're suggesting that a violent pop culture causes violent activity, then when we follow that suggestion to logical conclusions, there shouldn't be a single person alive in Japan. And I know that joke may seem fairly broad and easy, but like every joke there's a kernel of truth in it; the extremes of some Japanese pop culture are far more violent than any American equivalent. Cultural conservatives on the Right and Left, though, can't explain why the gun-toting action of some anime and films like *Battle Royale* isn't being recreated in the streets of Tokyo on a regular basis.

Violence and the Second Amendment

I didn't grow up in America, so I have no great or grand investment in the Second Amendment as an iconic principle of the American character. However, I'm in the process of becoming an American citizen, and I've been able to read English for a long time, so I feel like I have as much right to assert my position on the matter as any taxpayer. The Second Amendment protects the right to keep and bear arms for the purposes of a well-regulated militia. (And, much like some of the other language in the Bill of Rights, the times have changed; in my neighborhood, I'm more worried about getting tagged with a stray bullet than I am about British soldiers.) In a perfect world (which is to say, my perfect world and not yours), if you're a private citizen who'd like to own a gun, great; join the National Guard. You'll have access to it when you're on maneuvers and deployed. Otherwise, you don't. And as for hunters and rural farmers who "need" firearms, I'd be willing to make a compromise for them: They can own one single-shot bolt-action long rifle with no magazine whose ballistic signature is already on file at the local police station—which would also be the only place you can buy and store your bullets. (I once had a lengthy discussion about this with a cabbie in Vegas who was an avid hunter; when I suggested that if he truly loved hunting he could enjoy it just as much with a bow and arrow or single-shot bolt-action rifle, he countered that he wanted more firepower than that, because "I hate to see animals suffer." "Well," I noted with careful timing as we arrived at my destination, "then *maybe* you shouldn't be shooting them.")

Other than that? Stop selling guns, stop selling ammo— smash the molds and melt the inventory, with a very short amnesty period for people to turn their guns in, after which possession of a gun, never mind use, brings a life sentence. And I know this penalizes 'law-abiding' gun owners—but, seeing as how robberies and thefts from 'law-abiding' gun owners are how so many murder weapons come into the hands of criminals or the mentally ill, I don't have a lot of sympathy for that as an argument or a philosophical principle. Maybe you could talk me into seeing things that way. Maybe my thoughts about guns are a bunch of crazy jibber-jabber, and you can explain to me why they're naïve or impractical. I don't know. At least we'd be talking about it.

Having the Wrong Discussion

But when tragic events like the NIU shooting happen, we *don't* talk about the guns. We talk about the media, or the killer going off their medicines, or how there were no warning signs or how there were plenty of warning signs. My jaw dropped at a quote in a story about the NIU shooting, as Internet gun seller Eric Thompson, who also sold equipment to the Virginia Tech shooter [student Seung-Hui Cho, who killed thirty-two people and wounded many others in a rampage on April 16, 2007], expressed his shock after learning his store had sold Glock magazines and a holster to NIU shooter Steven Kazmierczak: "I'm still blown away by the coincidences. I'm shaking. I can't believe somebody would order from us again and do this." You sell gun accessories, and yet you can't believe someone would use them to do what they're made for? And if you're so shaken, why are you still in business?

No, guns don't kill people. But they make it a lot easier to do so, especially at a moment's notice as the result of some insane impulse; we can't legislate against someone wanting to pick up a gun, but we can make it less easy for them to have one, or four, or more at hand when they reach out for one. And gun companies don't kill people; they just make a lot of money as their products are used to kill people. If Kazmierczak had stepped into that class with a golf club or a knife or a baseball bat or a length of chain, many would still be hurt and some might still be dead. But he stepped into that class with three pistols and a shotgun, all of them legally obtained, and it makes me nauseated and ashamed that the first unbidden reaction I had to the NIU shootings was that five victims and the killer's own suicide seemed like a 'low' death count. And yes, we need better mental health funding in this country, so that the cracks people slip through are smaller. And we need to have constant serious discussions about what our entertainment says about us, and what that means. But at some point, someone—I don't know who, but I strongly doubt it'll be any of the current presidential candidates, some of whom would rather offer prayers and more prayers than policy initiatives, some of whom would rather write books instead of laws— someone needs to stand up and say that the very American principle of private gun ownership is leading to a very American practice of murder and tragedy. Mr. Pritchard and Mr. Thompson and others on the Right and Left suggest we need to look at the "culture of violence." But we've been talking about the culture of violence in relation to mass shootings for years and years now; when do we start *really* talking about guns?

5

Violent Video Games Might Be to Blame for Violent Behavior

Mark and Keisha Hoerrner

Mark Hoerrner is a writer and the author of several articles on the media's effect on children. Keisha Hoerrner is department chair of Kennesaw State University's First-Year Programs and a researcher who specializes in children and media issues.

While many parents scoff at letting their children watch violent movies, they often consent to buying violent video games for their teenagers without checking the industry ratings. Researchers contend that a link exists between violent video games and real-life violence in teenagers and young adults. Violent images don't necessarily create violent children, but gamers learn that violence is an accepted means to solve problems, and they perfect shooting skills as though they were handling real weapons. Even though games can teach children valuable coordination skills, parents and caregivers need to make sure that their children only view age-appropriate content and are made aware of the difference between on-screen actions and socially acceptable behavior in the real world.

Thomas has a 21-inch flat-screen monitor and an optimized computer with a 4 GHZ processing speed. His hard drive is fast and large; he's packed in close to three gigabytes of RAM and has a video card with dual 512K processors. It's

Mark and Keisha Hoerrner, "Video Game Violence," *Children's Voice*, vol. 15, January/February 2006. Copyright © 2006 Child Welfare League of America. All Rights Reserved. Reproduced by permission.

all about speed and graphical processing. He's jacked in to a high-speed Internet connection, and he's off and running.

Thomas isn't a programmer or a network engineer, though he's considering that as a possibility for the future. He doesn't have to worry about that now, though—he's only 13 years old and has a long time to make up his mind about a career. For now, he's content with the fact that in the next three hours, he'll commit 147 felonies including aggravated assault, murder, attempted murder, robbery, arson, burglary, conspiracy, assault with a deadly weapon, drug trafficking, and auto theft while violating just about every section of the RICO Act, the nation's anti–organized crime law. He'll even be so brazen as to gun down bystanders and police officers and will personally beat someone to death with a golf club.

All without ever leaving his room.

The Evolution of Video Games

The entire video game industry has changed dramatically since the days of *Pong*, where competitors sat through the rough-and-tumble world of a pixilated square bouncing between two rectangles in a tennis-like match of reflex and skill. Although that game was considered high tech just 30 years ago, the games today are vast and dazzling environments that seek to create an "immersive experience" for the player. Games like *EverQuest*, *World of Warcraft*, *Asheron's Call*, *Lineage II*, and *Star Wars Galaxies* have developed massive online, ever-changing settings that range from futuristic swamps, to steamy jungles and rainforests, to arid deserts.

Futuristic and fantastic settings aren't the only options— vast cityscapes in games like *City of Heroes*, and more realistic environments reflecting an expansive version of California, such as in the game *Grand Theft Auto: San Andreas*, are also available.

The common thread in all of these games is that the player is role-playing a character, determining everything from the outfits he or she wears to the way in which the character interacts with the online world and other players. These games range from single-player to thousand-plus multiplayer in which all players are in the online world simultaneously through a clever grouping of a large number of servers, all processing their whereabouts.

Just as children can improve their phonics with Learn to Read with Winnie the Pooh, *they can learn to shoot with deadly accuracy playing* Doom, Splinter Cell, Hitman, *and other first-person shooter games.*

Although these games can be highly entertaining, and they showcase some of the best qualities and abilities of the gaming industry, concern is growing over their violent content. *Grand Theft Auto: San Andreas* represents the extreme when it comes to violence, but many have a cartoon-like quality, such as the very popular *World of Warcraft*. They all share one goal—kill as many creatures as possible to gain rewards.

A Link to Violent Behavior

Retired Lt. Col. Dave Grossman, a former [U.S.] Army Ranger and tactical trainer, asserts that video games are actively training children to kill. Learning, he says, happens all the time, especially during active play. The subject of that active play, however, can be negative or positive.

Grossman has authored two books on the connection between violent media and actual violence. He argues that children learn to use weapons and become sharpshooters through simulated games the same way soldiers use simulations to improve their shooting precision. Just as children can improve their phonics with *Learn to Read with Winnie the Pooh*, they can learn to shoot with deadly accuracy playing *Doom*, *Splinter Cell*, *Hitman*, and other first-person shooter games.

Grossman has been a consultant to a number of school systems following deadly shooting incidents, assisting with grief counseling and understanding what brings children from what should be a carefree time in their lives to the point of committing multiple murders. In his book, *Stop Teaching Our Kids to Kill[: A Call to Action Against TV, Movie & Video Game Violence]*, Grossman says that in 1997's high school shooting in Paducah, Kentucky, the 14-year-old who opened fire on a before-school prayer group landed eight out of eight shots on eight different targets. Five of those were head shots [gunshot wounds to the head].

According to the FBI, in shootouts less than three meters from their targets, trained law enforcement officers land, on average, one out of five shots—these are trained officers who are familiar with their weapons.

The teenage shooter had never held a real gun before his shooting rampage, Grossman says. He had, however, spent long hours playing first-person shooter games that simulated killing with the same weapon he used that morning. Grossman, who now travels the country talking to police departments and educators, asserts that the combination of playing these games and watching violent movies taught the youth how to load, actively target, and shoot as if he had been watching an instructional video.

Making Right or Wrong Choices

Unlike watching a video or television show, a child is actively making choices and weighing options when playing video games. He or she is rewarded for certain behaviors, which, depending on the game, may range from solving a puzzle to opening fire on a group of bystanders.

"In a violent video game, you rehearse the entire aggression sequence from beginning to end," says media violence researcher Craig [A.] Anderson, chair of Iowa State University's Department of Psychology. "You have to be vigilant, looking for enemies, looking for potential threats; you have to decide how to deal with the threat, what weapon to use, and how to use it; and then you take physical action to behave aggressively within the game.

It's society, not science, that must decide how to deal with the negative effects of violent video games.

"We have considerable evidence these games cause violent behavior," Anderson says, pointing to hundreds of scientific studies on video games, and more than 3,000 on the effects of other violent media, that he says all suggest a causal link between violent behavior and the consumption of violent content. This isn't an overt link, he cautions—a child isn't likely to go out and commit a major felony after playing a violent game for an hour—but children will act more aggressively and show more negative social action, such as the intent to do violence to another person, over time.

Positive Aspects of Video Games

Anderson is quick to note, however, that games have positive aspects. He bought his son a copy of the flight simulator game *Flight Unlimited* and a realistic joystick and foot pedal. His son spent considerable time learning to fly, which paid off when the child went to a NASA summer camp and was assigned the role of pilot on a space shuttle mission simulator. Anderson's son was able to land the craft on the first try, something camp organizers said had never been done. Anderson credits the flight simulator as the catalyst for helping his son develop the necessary skills.

In a study at the University of California, Santa Barbara, diabetic children who received a video game showing them how to better manage their illness had improved blood sugar control and fewer emergency room visits. "Video games are great teachers and great motivators," Anderson says, "but they can be misused. It's society, not science, that must decide how to deal with the negative effects of violent video games."

To this end, the video game industry helped create the Entertainment Software Rating Board (ESRB) to develop a system of ratings for video games to define content for parents and allow them to make informed purchasing decisions. ESRB ratings include six age-based rating symbols, ranging from "EC-Early Childhood" to "AO-Adults Only," and more than 30 content descriptors (such as "Mild Violence," "Intense Violence," "Sexual Violence," "Partial Nudity," "Drug Reference," and "Simulated Gambling") that indicate elements in a game that may have triggered a particular rating or may be of interest or concern to the buyer.

The Impact of Ratings

Although the rating system is comprehensive, some recent studies raise the question of whether parents rely on or ignore the ratings. In a study by Peter D. Hart Research Associates, 78% of parents said they were aware of the rating system, 70% said they check the ESRB rating for age appropriateness when buying computer and video games for their children "every time" or "most of the time," and 54% said they check the content descriptors.

On the other hand, according to a [Henry J.] Kaiser [Family] Foundation study of media habits of youth and families, among 11- to 14-year-olds, 75% of parents set no limits about what video games their children could play. For teens ages 15–18, the lack of parental supervision on content jumped to 95%.

The irony is that most of these parents would be leery of letting their teen watch a movie with an R or NC-17 rating, yet they seem to have no qualms about buying a video game for their children with an M [Mature] rating or higher.

Barry Ritholtz of the Webzine *The Big Picture* reports that last year, U.S. sales of video games topped $7 billion, giving video game producers a huge incentive for turning out more and more engaging games. Even more lucrative is the growing market for online games. The market research firm DFC Intelligence Group has projected that by 2009, the online game market will generate just under $10 billion annually. Most console games, such as those made for Nintendo and PlayStation, are one-shot purchases. Online gamers, however, not only pay $40–$50 per game to get started, but often fork over as much as $15 per month to play games.

Game developers display an almost cavalier attitude in creating software.

The Question of Content

Within this massive market, researchers like Anderson say there should be some degree of accountability for game manufacturers. Yet, despite its promotion of the ESRB rating system as a comprehensive tool for parents, the Video Software Dealers Association has waged an intense legal campaign against any legislative limits on the content of games, even when legislation corresponds directly to the industry's voluntary ratings.

Game developers display an almost cavalier attitude in creating software. Recently, the makers of *Grand Theft Auto: San Andreas* came under fire from U.S. Senator Hillary Rodham Clinton (D-NY), who publicly condemned the game's developer, Rockstar Games, when gamers uncovered hidden objectionable sexual content within the game. Many games, especially those for home computers, can be altered through third-party modification software—"mods"—that allows users to create customized content for a game. Teenagers using mods discovered strong sexual scenes hidden within *San An-*

dreas. The sexual content wasn't created with third-party software; it was already resident in the original retail game.

In response, ESRB immediately changed the game's M rating to AO (Adults Only). What followed was the only show of public power the market has retained—many stores refuse to carry AO-rated titles, and the game was yanked from store shelves nationwide.

With a growing surge of violent games on the market, parents and child advocates need to know how to keep children out of the less prosocial aspects of the video game industry and concentrate on getting children into games that offer fun and challenging scenarios. . . .

As MediaWise founder David Walsh says, "The storytellers define the culture." Parents, teachers, social workers, and child advocates need to clearly understand the stories being told in video games, because the line between fiction and reality will continue to blur.

6

Violent Video Games Are Not to Blame for Violent Behavior

Daniel Koffler

Daniel Koffler is a contributor to Reason *and was* Reason's *2005 Burton C. Gray Memorial Intern.*

Since the tragedy of the Columbine High School shootings in 1999, it has become a commonly held belief that video games play a role in school violence. While political figures are eager to condemn video games, they fail to take into account the other violent entertainment options that are readily available to children. Politicians and video game prohibitionists not only rely on an emotional appeal when they present evidence linking video games to violent youth, but they are also very selective in the evidence they impart.

In May, by a vote of 106 to 6, the Illinois legislature passed a measure banning the sale of "violent" and "sexually explicit" video games to minors. The California Assembly is considering its own version of a prohibition on game sales to the underaged, and Washington, Indiana, and Missouri already have enacted similar laws, only to see them struck down on First Amendment grounds.

Video games are an appealing target for a public figure in search of a crusade. Movies and music have energetic advocates, but it's hard to find anyone who will defend games for their artistic value, or even on the on the grounds of freedom

Daniel Koffler, "Grand Theft Scapegoat: The Ridiculous Jihad Against Video Games," *Reason*, October 2005.

of expression. Usually the strongest argument made for games is that they are harmless fun. That's not the most effective response when the governor of Illinois is claiming "too many of the video games marketed to our children teach them all of the wrong lessons and all of the wrong values."

There is no shortage of readily available literature on the relationship between media exposure and behavior, and the evidence does not support the prohibitionists' case.

Ominously, the Illinois proposal pays no heed to the existing range of voluntary content ratings, which run from EC ("Early Childhood") to AO ("Adults Only") and ostensibly allow game merchants to decide for themselves what constitutes "violent" or "sexually explicit" material. In a message "to the parents of Illinois," Democratic Gov. Rod Blagojevich asserts that "ninety-eight percent of the games considered suitable by the industry for teenagers contain graphic violence." Blagojevich is surely abusing language and statistics—if you stretch the phrase far enough, even the mild-mannered *Super Mario Bros.* includes what could be described as "graphic violence"—but the implication is that the proposed legislation's content restrictions could apply to games the ratings board approved for teens.

Selective Evidence

It would not be fair to say that the arguments for video game criminalization are completely uncontaminated by evidence. But prohibitionists are highly selective about the evidence they present and are careless once they've presented it, hoping to substitute raw emotional appeal for a plausible explanatory framework. Blagojevich, for example, claims "experts have found that exposure to violent video games increases aggressive thoughts, feelings, and behaviors"—as if no more need be said about the causal relationship between playing video games and engaging in antisocial behavior. Such rhetoric implies that video game players are empty, infinitely corruptible ciphers.

There is no shortage of readily available literature on the relationship between media exposure and behavior, and the evidence does not support the prohibitionists' case. A 2004 study of "Short-Term Psychological and Cardiovascular Effects on Habitual Players," conducted by researchers at the University of Bologna, concluded that "owning video games does not in fact seem to have negative effects on aggressive human behavior." A 2004 report in the *Journal of the American Medical Association* noted: "If video games do increase violent tendencies outside the laboratory, the explosion of gaming over the past decade from $3.2 billion in sales in 1995 to $7 billion in 2003, according to industry figures, would suggest a parallel trend in youth violence. Instead, youth violence has been decreasing."

What separates efforts to curb children's exposure to video games from older, parallel campaigns is how profoundly out of touch they are with the realities of the entertainment choices available to children.

Likewise, criminologist Joanne Savage contends in a 2004 issue of *Aggression and Violent Behavior* that "there is little evidence in favor of focusing on media violence as a means of remedying our violent crime problem." In the absence of a wave of real-life, game-inspired carnage, Harvard Medical School psychiatry professor Cheryl Olson, writing in the journal *Academic Psychiatry* in the summer of 2004, advised that "it's time to move beyond blanket condemnations and frightening anecdotes and focus on developing targeted educational and policy interventions based on solid data."

Unfortunately, blanket condemnations and frightening anecdotes are likely to be with us as long as they prove electorally profitable. In March, Sens. Hillary Clinton (D-N.Y.), Joseph Lieberman (D-Conn.), Sam Brownback (R-Kan.), and Rick Santorum (R-Pa.) jointly proposed a $90 million appropriation to study the effects of games and other media on children. Apparently, no one on any of the senators' staffs could be bothered to point out that there already is plenty of credible research on precisely that question. Either that, or a bipartisan coalition of presidential aspirants calculated that bashing game designers could be a cheap way to endear themselves to family-values voters.

Entertainment Choices Available to Children

This is hardly the first time politicians have attempted to bludgeon popular culture into submission. (Recall the political grandstanding that followed past moral panics over movies, comic books, and rock music.) What separates efforts to curb children's exposure to video games from older, parallel campaigns is how profoundly out of touch they are with the realities of the entertainment choices available to children.

For example, Hillary Clinton—fresh from her collaboration with Santorum and Brownback, and consistent with her advertised principle of "fighting the culture of sex and violence in the media"—decided in mid-July to intervene in the controversy over the "Hot Coffee" mod for the game *Grand Theft Auto: San Andreas* [*GTA*]. Hot Coffee is a hidden component of the game's coding that, if unlocked via a program that can be freely downloaded from the Internet, will treat a player to scenes of grainy, polygonal sex. Outraged, Clinton wrote a letter to the Federal Trade Commission urging it to investigate whether Rockstar (the company that produces *GTA*) created the Hot Coffee content. She seemed oblivious to one of the first lessons a new Web surfer learns: There is a universe of free Internet pornography that anyone looking online for explicit sex can see without bothering to download and install a video game modification.

The sheer scope of media choices renders futile any effort to rein in content through regulations. Occasional pixilated displays of violence and sex can be found in some games that are sometimes sold to children. (Sixteen percent of games are rated "Mature," and 16 percent of game buyers are under 18, according to the Entertainment Software Association.) These comprise a tiny part of the total array of media content freely available to anyone.

Legislators nevertheless are drafting self-righteous bills that practically beg to be overturned in court. With any luck, that will keep the prohibitionists occupied until they discover the next dire threat to our children.

7

Violent Video Games Are Harmful to Young People

William Sears

William Sears is a physician and the author of over thirty books on child care. He is an associate clinical professor of pediatrics at the School of Medicine at the University of California, Irvine.

Video games have become a major player in the entertainment industry, while also becoming increasingly violent. The correlation between violent content and real-life aggression has been long established and video games condition children to act violently. The long hours children spend playing violent video games teach them to solve problems with aggressive behavior and make them fearful of a world that seems to be marked by aggression and brutality.

Video games may be hazardous to your child's emotional health.

Sounds like a warning on a cigarette pack, and justifiably so. Once upon a time TV was blamed for a variety of children's emotional disturbances, from obesity to aggression. Just as parents learned to tame the TV, along came another electronic influence that can undermine a child's success far more than television. . . .

Disturbing Statistics

Video games are becoming the second largest segment of the entertainment industry, second to television. Around half of all children have a video game player or a computer on which to play the games in their own bedrooms. A study comparing parental rules for television viewing and playing video games showed that parents set rules for video games only half as much as they do for TV viewing, and the majority of parents did not restrict the type of games their children played. Eighty percent of the most popular video games feature aggressiveness or violence as the primary themes, and in twenty percent of these games the aggressiveness or violence is directed toward women. Surveys conclude that on a typical day, one in four American boys plays an extremely violent video game. And the sales of extremely violent games are climbing. By the time typical American children reach the age of eighteen, they have seen 200,000 acts of violence and 40,000 murders on some sort of screen.

Many, many studies have shown a definite correlation between the degree of violence in video game viewing and the degree of aggressive behavior in the viewing children. In his book *Stop Teaching Our Kids to Kill[: A Call to Action Against TV, Movie & Video Game Violence]*, [retired] Lieutenant Colonel David Grossman, a psychologist at Arkansas State University and past specialist as a "killologist," points out that willingness to kill another person is not a natural behavior, but one that has to be taught by repeated desensitization and exposure to violence. He goes on to reveal that part of teaching soldiers to kill demands a conditioned response so that shooting a gun becomes automatic. According to Lieutenant Colonel Grossman, the Marine Corps uses modified versions of grossly violent video games (like the ones that allegedly motivated the Columbine carnage [when high school students Eric Harris and Dylan Klebold killed fifteen and injured twenty-four others at Columbine High School in Colorado on April 20, 1999]) to teach recruits how to kill. These are used to develop the "will to kill" by repeatedly rehearsing the act until it feels natural. Obviously, this technology is much more dangerous in the hands of kids than among soldiers and police. Grossman refers to violent video games as "murder simulators." . . .

Conditioning Children to Be Violent

Children are not born violent, they are made violent. They become conditioned to associate violence with fun, as part of "normal life." Are we bringing up a generation of soldiers, or are we bringing up children? The end result of unmonitored video violence is we are training an army of kids. There is a psychological and physiological principle called "operant conditioning," which is a stimulus-response training where a person is conditioned to act, not think, in a stressful situation. This is how pilots train in flight simulators and the U.S. Army trains its soldiers. Could the video game addict become conditioned to shoot or hit whenever provoked? Could these video games trigger what we call "instant replay," so that the player is conditioned to pull a trigger when seeing someone go after his girlfriend? We are concerned that this terrifying technology can fill a child's vulnerable and receptive brain with a whole library of scary instant replays, so that by reflex he replays one of these violent scenes when faced with a real-life problem.

Children instinctively copy adult behavior, and violent imagery is much more easily stored in the memory than less violent behavior.

Kids are becoming increasingly attracted to violence and numb to its consequences. They build up an immunity to violence and therefore need higher levels of violence as "booster shots." Since violence is actually unnatural for children, video games make it fun for them, which gradually conditions the child to believe that violence is natural. Lieutenant Colonel Grossman dubs this as AVIDS—acquired violence immune deficiency syndrome. As violence goes on to desensitize children, they perceive violence as "cool." At a very young age, children learn to associate violence with pleasure and excitement, a dangerous association for a civilized society. As the desensitization process continues, parents should be aware of disturbing words, such as "It's just a game," or the most concerning, "It doesn't bother me." It should bother them.

Blurring the Border Between Fantasy and Reality

Children instinctively copy adult behavior, and violent imagery is much more easily stored in the memory than less violent behavior. Yet, many preteen children have not yet learned to completely differentiate fantasy from reality. They view, interact and get involved with the video game, yet developmentally lack the moral judgments as to the rightness or wrongness of the action. They lack discernment. Violent screens put the wrong messages into children's vulnerable brains at the wrong time.

The "hype hormones" that are aroused by violent video games cause children to suffer serious consequences, such as nightmares, headaches, anorexia, and fatigue. Some studies have even related seizure activity to violent screen time. Violent video games have been found to stress the cardiovascular system, such as increasing blood pressure and rapid breathing characteristic of a physiologic stress response. One study even reported an increase in the stress hormone adrenaline during video playing. A 1998 study showed that while playing video games, children experience a high release of the brain neurotransmitter dopamine, which could be called the hype hormone.

During TV watching, children are just passive viewers of screen violence, yet with video games they can interact. With the push of a button or click of a mouse they can point and shoot, kill, and squash—and they get more points for more killing. Video arcades are even worse. There is no parental monitoring and the joysticks are more like guns, enabling children to point and shoot. In some violent programs on TV, at least the bad consequences of violence are often pointed out, and the bad guy often loses. On the contrary, with video games the bad guy often wins, or at least gets to a "higher level." In fact, the violent characters are often more glamorized in video games than on television. With TV watching, many little brains just tune out, yet with video games teens often tune up. Instead of watching killings, the player can kill.

The Game Addiction

Over sixty percent of children report that they play video games longer than they had intended to play. Once they get engrossed in a game, they get hooked on the hype and want to play longer. The games fit into the natural desire for children to get control over their lives, and video games give children a feeling of mastery that they may not have over other aspects of their lives. Playing violent video games is like a drug. Once the child reaches a certain level of violence and becomes bored—what is known physiologically as habituated—the child needs more of the "drug" to maintain the high level of excitement.

The most disturbing fact is that children who have the least amount of self-esteem and mastery over their life are the ones most attracted to video games. According to Dr. Jane Healy in her book *Endangered Minds[: Why Children Don't Think and What We Can Do About It]*, boys who pursue violent video games are more likely to have low self-confidence in school and be less successful in personal relationships. Studies have also shown that for girls increased time playing video or computer games is associated with lowered self-esteem. These games give children an out when they don't feel in with other groups.

Role-playing games (RPGs) allow children to play the role of violent characters. The roles of these characters become more attractive to the children, especially if they don't like their roles in the world they live in. Children learn that violent characters are cool, powerful, and in some misguided way, successful. During video playing, children get instant gratification and can manipulate their roles to what they want. Yet, in the real world, they have to wait, and it's not always fun.

Violent video games distort a child's perception of the real world as violent and fearful.

A Fearful World

It's the nature of a growing child to view the world as a kind and safe place to live. Violent video games distort a child's perception of the real world as violent and fearful. Media researchers fear that children will grow up viewing the world as violent and dangerous—a viewpoint dubbed the mean world syndrome.

Many pediatricians rank screen violence as a public health issue at the same level as smoking and cancer. In fact, the American Academy of Pediatrics advises doctors to take a "media history" during annual checkups on school-age children. Here is one graphic example: Scary technology now allows players to "morph" head shots [portraits] of other people (such as other kids or teachers whom they might hate) onto the bodies of the characters in the video game in order to shoot their heads off.

Condemnations of Media Violence Are Often Simplistic and Misguided

Henry Jenkins

Henry Jenkins is the director of the Massachusetts Institute of Technology's Comparative Media Studies Program and is the Peter de Florez Professor of Humanities. He is the author and editor of nine books on various aspects of media and popular culture, including Textual Poachers: Television Fans and Participatory Culture, Hop on Pop: The Politics and Pleasures of Popular Culture *and* From Barbie to Mortal Kombat: Gender and Computer Games. *His newest books include* Convergence Culture: Where Old and New Media Collide *and* Fans, Bloggers, and Gamers: Exploring Participatory Culture.

The discussions about media violence and whether it does or does not cause young people to act aggressively are largely misguided, because no common definition of the term exists. Violence comes in very different forms—implied violence, news about violent occurrences, war movies, fairy tales, nature programs, and shooting games—and is dealt with in many different ways. It is nonsensical to assume that people who commit violent crimes have learned their aggression via watching television or playing video games, since even children have an understanding of the difference between real violence and symbolic representa-

Henry Jenkins, "A Few Thoughts on Media Violence . . .," Confessions of an Aca-Fan: The Official Weblog of Henry Jenkins, April 25, 2007. www.henryjenkins.org. Reproduced by permission of the author.

tions of aggression. Instead our society should engage in an intelligent discussion about the nature of aggression and the ways in which media present violence to provoke us or to simply entertain.

The news of last week's tragic shooting at Virginia Tech [when student Seung-Hui Cho killed thirty-two people and wounded many others on April 16, 2007] has brought the usual range of media reformers and culture warriors (never camera shy) scurrying back into the public eye to make their case that "media violence" must be contained, if not censored, if we are to prevent such bloodshed from occurring again. Almost immediately, longtime video game opponents Jack Thompson and Dr. Phil McGraw started appearing on television talk shows, predicting that the shooter would turn out to be a hard-core video game player. (The odds are certainly with them since a study released several years ago of frosh at 20 American colleges and universities found that a hundred percent of them had played games before going off to college and that on average college students spend more time each week playing games than reading recreationally, watching television, or going to the movies.) In fact, when the police searched the killer's dorm room, they found not a single game nor any signs of a game system.

Misleading Discussions Abound

The focus then quickly shifted, with the news arguing first that the shooter was a heavy viewer of television "including television wrestling" and then linking some of the photographs he sent to NBC with images from Asian cult cinema—most notably with the Korean film *Old Boy*. An op-ed piece in the *Washington Post* asserted that *Old Boy* "must feature prominently in the discussion" of Mr. [Seung-Hui] Cho's possible motivations, "even if no one has yet confirmed that Cho saw it," and then later claims that Cho "was shooting a John Woo movie in his head" as he entered the engineering building.

And then, of course, there was that damning evidence that he had constructed violent and aggressive fantasies during his creative writing classes. *Time* magazine even pathologizes the fact that he was a college student who *didn't* have a Facebook page! Talk about damned if you do and damned if you don't!

None of this should surprise us given the cycle of media coverage that has surrounded previous instances of school shootings. An initial period of shock is quickly followed by an effort to round up the usual suspects and hold them accountable—this is part of the classic psychology of a moral panic. In an era of 24-hour news, the networks already have experts on media violence in their speed dial, ready for them to arrive on the scene and make the same old arguments. As a media scholar, I find these comments predictable but disappointing: disappointing because they block us from having a deeper conversation about the place of violence in American culture.

Our culture tells lots of different stories about violence for lots of different reasons for lots of different audiences in lots of different contexts.

I want to outline here another set of perspectives on the issue of media violence, ones that are grounded not in the literature of media effects but rather in the literature of cultural studies. I have plenty of criticisms of the media effects approach . . . , but for the most part, my focus here is more on what cultural studies might tell us about media violence than it is in critiquing that body of "research."

A Different Perspective

So, let me start with an intentionally provocative statement. There is no such thing as media violence—at least not in the ways that we are used to talking about it—as something which can be easily identified, counted, and studied in the laboratory. Media violence is not something that exists outside of a specific cultural and social context. It is not one thing which we can simply eliminate from art and popular culture. It's not a problem we can make go away. Our culture tells lots of different stories about violence for lots of different reasons for lots of different audiences in lots of different contexts. We need to stop talking about media violence in the abstract and start talking about it in much more particularized terms.

Otherwise, we end up looking pretty silly. So, for example, a study endorsed by the American Academy of Pediatrics reported that 100 percent of feature-length cartoons released in America between 1937 and 1999 contained images of violence. Here, we see the tendency to quantify media violence taken to its logical extreme. For this statement to be true, violence has to be defined here so broadly that it would include everything from the poison apple in *Snow White* to the hunter who shoots Bambi's mother, from Captain Hook's hook to the cobra that threatens to crush Mowgli in *The Jungle Book* and that's just to stick with the Disney canon. The definition must include not only physical violence but threats of violence, implied violence, and psychological/emotional violence. Indeed, if we start from a definition that broad, we would need to eliminate conflict from our drama altogether in order to shut down the flow of media violence into our culture. Perhaps this is reason enough not to put pediatricians in charge of our national cultural policy anytime soon. Certainly few of us would imagine our culture improved if these films were stripped of their "violent" content or barred from exhibition.

The Problem of Defining Violence

Almost no one operates on a definition of violence that broad. Most of us make value judgments about the kinds of violence that worry us, judgments based on the meanings attached to the violence in specific representations, so church groups don't think twice about sending young kids to watch Jesus get beaten in *The Passion of the Christ*, and games reformers go after first-person shooters but not World War II simulation games (which coat their violence in patriotism and historical authenticity) even though this genre is now consistently out-selling more antisocial titles in the video game marketplace.

Why is violence so persistent in our popular culture? Because violence has been persistent as a theme across storytelling media of all kinds. A thorough account of violence in media would include: fairy tales such as "Hansel and Gretel," oral epics such as Homer's *The Iliad*, the staged violence of Shakespeare's plays, fine art paintings of the Rape of the Sabine Women, and stained-glass window representations of saints being crucified or pumped full of arrows, or for that matter, talk show conversations about the causes of school shootings. If we were to start going after media violence, then we would need to throw out much of the literary canon and close down all of our art museums. Violence is fundamental to these various media because aggression and conflict are core aspects of human experience. We need our art to help us make sense of the senselessness of violence in the real world, to provide some moral order, to help us sort through our feelings, to provoke us to move beyond easy answers and ask hard questions.

We have, for the most part, moved from an era where humans sought entertainment through actual violence and into a period when we are amused through symbolic violence.

Again, nobody really means that we should get rid of all media violence, even if that's what they say often enough: We are all drawing lines and making distinctions, but all of those distinctions fly out the window when we read statistics that count the number of incidents of violence in an hour of television or when we read research that tells us how subjecting human lab rats to media violence may make them more or less aggressive.

In practice, it is hard to sustain the case that our culture is becoming more violent—not when we read it within the broader sweep of human history. Take a look at Robert Darnton's *The Great Cat Massacre*, which describes how workers in early modern Europe got their kicks by setting cats on fire and running them through the streets. Consider the role of public hangings in 19th-century America. Or think about the popularity of cockfights and bearbaiting in Shakespeare's London. We have, for the most part, moved from an era where humans sought entertainment through actual violence and into a period when we are amused through symbolic violence. Indeed, where people confront real violence on a regular basis, parents are often heartened to see their children playing violent video games—if for no other reason than they keep them off the streets and out of harm's way. (This is borne out by studies done in American ghettos or along the West Bank.)

Violence in the Media Is Global

Nor can we argue that America is unique in its fascination with violent entertainment. I recently took a trip to Singapore and visited Haw Par Villa, a cherished institution, where tourists can go into the mouth of hell and see grisly images of doomed souls being ground up, decapitated and dismembered, and impaled, drenched with buckets of red paint. For generations, Singaporeans have taken their children to this attraction for moral instruction, showing their young and impressionable ones what befalls those who lie to their parents or cheat on their examinations.

Our current framing of media violence assumes that it . . . attracts us, that it inspires imitation, whereas throughout much of human history, representations of violence were seen as morally instructive, as making it less likely we are going to transgress various social prohibitions. When we read the lives of saints, for example, we are invited to identify with the one suffering the violence and not the one committing it.

Media violence is not a uniquely American trend, though school shootings, by and large, are. Media violence is a global phenomenon. Indeed, the process of globalization is arguably increasing the vividness with which violence is represented not only in American media but in every major media-producing country. The physicality of violent representations is easily conveyed visually, allowing it to be understood and appreciated by people who might miss the nuances of spoken dialogue, who might not understand the language in which the film was produced or be able to read the subtitles. For that reason, action stars are often the most popular performers in the global market. As the United States, Japan, China, India, Korea, and a host of other film-producing countries compete for dominance in the global marketplace, we are seeing an escalation in the intensity of representations of violence. And American media often seem mild when compared with the kinds of things that can be found on screens in Asia or Latin America.

There's a kind of deadening literal-mindedness about such criticisms: to represent something is to advocate it and to advocate it is to cause it.

Imitating Art

Part of the problem with the initial response to the news of the Virginia Tech shootings was the assumption that the young man involved would turn out to be a fan of American media violence. In fact, the evidence so far suggests that he was much more interested in Asian cinema, which should hardly be a surprise given that he came to the United States from Korea. Indeed, the news media have more recently noted similarities between his two-handed shooting techniques and the style made famous by Hong Kong action director John Woo;

they have also identified one of the images—where he waves a hammer—with a publicity still for the Korean film *Old Boy*.

A news story in the *New York Times* describes *Old Boy* as an obscure cult film, which appeals primarily to those who are interested in excessive violence. In fact, *Old Boy* has emerged as one of the most important films in the recent Korean film revival, one which has won awards from film festivals and has been playing in art houses across the country. While the film includes some of the most disturbing violence I've seen on screen in some time, that's precisely the point: The violence is meant to be disturbing. We watch the main character's slow descent into his own personal hell and then as he seeks to right wrongs that have been committed against him, we see him pushed into more and more violence himself. The film-maker doesn't glorify the violence: He's horrified by it; he's using it to push past our own reserves and to get us to engage in issues of oppression and social aggression from a fresh per-spective. I have always been struck by the fact that moral re-formers rarely take aim at mundane and banal representations of violence though formulaic violence is pervasive in our cul-ture. Almost always, they go after works that are acclaimed elsewhere as art—the works of Martin Scorsese or Quentin Tarantino, say—precisely because these works manage to get under their skin. For some of us, this provocation gets us thinking more deeply about the moral consequences of vio-lence whereas others condemn the works themselves, unable to process the idea that a work might provoke us to reflect about the violence that it represents.

There's a kind of deadening literal-mindedness about such criticisms: to represent something is to advocate it and to ad-vocate it is to cause it. To watch this film and decide to imi-tate the protagonist is a misreading on the order of reading *Frankenstein* and deciding to construct a creature from the parts of dead bodies or watching *A Clockwork Orange* and de-ciding it is fun to rape and terrorize senior citizens. It is certainly possible for someone who already is mentally disturbed to read these images out of context and ascribe to them meanings that are not part of the original but then again, that's part of the point.

Media Don't Cause Violence

If we take most of the existing research on media effects at face value, almost nothing would suggest that consuming media violence would turn an otherwise normal kid into a psycho killer. In practice, the research implies that consuming media violence can be one risk factor among many, that most incidents of real-world violence cannot be traced back to a single cause, and that real-world experiences (mental illness, drug abuse, histories of domestic violence, exposure to gangs, etc.) represent a much more immediate cause of most violent crime. Some research has shown that people in jail for violent crimes, in fact, consume less media violence than the general population, in part because they have not been able to afford consistent access to media technologies.

> *Clearly, those kids who already live in a culture of violence are often drawn most insistently to violent entertainment.*

Understanding media violence as a risk factor—rather than as the cause of real-world violence—is consistent with some of the other things we know or think we know about media's influence. At the risk of reducing this to a simple formula, media are most powerful when they reaffirm our existing beliefs and behaviors, least powerful when they seek to change them. We tend to read media representations against our perceptions of the real world and discard them if they deviate too dramatically from what we believe to be true.

In fact, children at a pretty young age—certainly by the time they reach elementary school—are capable of making at least crude distinctions between more or less realistic representations of violence. They can be fooled by media that offer ambiguous cues but they generally read media that seem realistic very differently than media that seem cartoonish or larger than life. For that reason, they are often much more emotionally disturbed by documentaries that depict predators and prey, war, or crime, than they are by the kinds of hyperbolic representations we most often are talking about when we refer to media violence.

The Context of Violence

None of this is to suggest that the media we consume have no effect. Clearly, those kids who already live in a culture of violence are often drawn most insistently to violent entertainment. They may seek to use it to release their pent-up anger and frustration; they may use its images to try to make sense of what they see as aggression and injustice around them; they may draw on its iconography to give some shape to their own inchoate feelings, and that's part of the way I would understand those disturbing photographs of Seung-Hui Cho striking poses from Asian action movies. We can't argue that these films had nothing to do with the horrors he committed on teachers and students at Virginia Tech. I think it does matter that he had access to some images of violence and not others and that he read those representations of violence through a set of emotional and psychological filters that distorted and amplified their messages.

Where does this leave us? It is meaningless, as I have suggested, to talk about regulating "media violence," as if all representations of violence were harmful. We need to get beyond rhetoric that treats media violence as a carcinogen, a poison or a pollutant. Rather, we should be asking ourselves what kinds of stories our culture tells about violence and how we are making sense of those representations in the context of our everyday lives. The problem is not media violence *per se*.

If there is a problem, it is that so many of our contemporary works banalize violence through reliance on simpleminded formulas. What we need is more meaningful violence—representations of violence that incite and provoke us to think more deeply about the nature of aggression, trauma, and loss, representations that get under our skin and make it hard for us to simply sit back and relax in front of the screen. And we need to be having intelligent conversations about these media constructions of violence rather than trying to push such works away from us.

9

Violent Media Do Not Teach a Christian Worldview

Kerby Anderson

Kerby Anderson is the national director of Probe Ministries International, an Evangelical Christian organization. He is the author of several books including Christian Ethics in Plain Language, Origin Science, *and* Signs of Warning, Signs of Hope.

Abundant studies have proven the negative effects of television on its viewers. Television sets are in nearly every household, and television content has grown ever more violent. Graphic violence is pervasive, and children especially become victims, displaying aggressive behavior in response to television brutality. The Bible teaches that what people view will become part of their being. Parents should curb television's influence and adopt a Christian perspective of the world.

Is there too much sex and violence on television? Most Americans seem to think so. One survey found that seventy-five percent of Americans felt that television had "too much sexually explicit material." Moreover, eighty-six percent believed that television had contributed to "a decline in values." And no wonder. Channel surfing through the television reveals plots celebrating premarital sex, adultery, and even homosexuality. Sexual promiscuity in the media appears to be at an all-time high. A study of adolescents (ages twelve to seventeen) showed that watching sex on TV influences teens to have sex. Youths were more likely to initiate intercourse as well as other sexual activities.

The Extent of the Problem

A study by the Parents Television Council found that prime-time network television is more violent than ever before. In addition, they found that this increasing violence is also of a sexual nature. They found that portrayals of violence are up seventy-five percent since 1998.

The study also provided expert commentary by Deborah [J.] Fisher, PhD. She states that children, on average, will be exposed to a thousand murders, rapes, and assaults per year through television. She goes on to warn that early exposure to television violence has "consistently emerged as a significant predictor of later aggression."

No longer can defenders of television say that TV is "not that bad." The evidence is in, and television is more offensive than ever.

A previous study by the Parents Television Council compared the changes in sex, language, and violence between decades. The special report entitled *What a Difference a Decade Makes* found many shocking things.

First, on a per-hour basis, sexual material more than tripled in the last decade. For example, while references to homosexuality were once rare, now they are mainstream. Second, the study found that foul language increased fivefold in just a decade. They also found that the intensity of violent incidents significantly increased.

These studies provide the best quantifiable measure of what has been taking place on television. No longer can defenders of television say that TV is "not that bad." The evidence is in, and television is more offensive than ever.

Christians should not be surprised by these findings. Sex and violence have always been part of the human condition because of our sin nature, but modern families are exposed to a level of sex and violence that is unprecedented. Obviously, this will have a detrimental effect. The Bible teaches that "as a man thinks in his heart, so is he." What we see and hear affects our actions. And while this is true for adults, it is especially true for children.

Television's Impact on Behavior

What is the impact of watching television on subsequent behavior? There are abundant studies that document that what you see, hear, and read does affect your perception of the world and your behavior.

The American Academy of Pediatrics in 2000 issued a "Joint Statement on the Impact of Entertainment Violence on Children." They cited over one thousand studies, including reports from the surgeon general's office and the National Institute of Mental Health. They say that these studies "point overwhelmingly to a causal connection between media violence and aggressive behavior in some children."

In 1992, the American Psychological Association concluded that forty years of research on the link between TV violence and real-life violence has been ignored, stating that "the 'scientific debate is over' and calling for federal policy to protect society."

Television is universally available, and thus has the most profound effect on our culture.

A 1995 poll of children ten to sixteen years of age showed that children recognize that "what they see on television encourages them to take part in sexual activity too soon, to show disrespect for their parents, to lie and to engage in aggressive behavior." More than two-thirds said they are influenced by television; seventy-seven percent said TV shows too much sex before marriage, and sixty-two percent said sex on television and in movies influences their peers to have sexual relations when they are too young. Two-thirds also cited certain programs featuring dysfunctional families as encouraging disrespect toward parents.

The report reminds us that television sets the baseline standard for the entire entertainment industry. Most homes (ninety-eight percent) have a television set. And according to recent statistics, that TV in the average household is on more than eight hours each day.

By contrast, other forms of entertainment (such as movies, DVDs, CDs) must be sought out and purchased. Television is universally available, and thus has the most profound effect on our culture.

As Christians we need to be aware of the impact television has on us and our families. The studies show us that sex and violence on TV can affect us in subtle yet profound ways. We can no longer ignore the growing body of data that suggests that televised imagery does affect our perceptions and behaviors. So we should be concerned about the impact television (as well as other forms of media) has on our neighbors and our society as a whole. . . .

Sex and Violence on Television

I have previously written about the subject of pornography and talked about the dangerous effects of sex, especially when linked with violence. Neil Malamuth and Edward Donnerstein document the volatile impact of sex and violence in the media. They say, "There can be relatively long-term, antisocial effects of movies that portray sexual violence as having positive consequences."

In a message given by Donnerstein, he concluded with this warning and observation: "If you take normal males and expose them to graphic violence against women in R-rated films, the research doesn't show that they'll commit acts of violence against women. It doesn't say they will go out and commit rape. But it does demonstrate that they become less sensitized to violence against women, they have less sympathy for rape victims, and their perceptions and attitudes and values about violence change."

It is important to remember that these studies are applicable not just to hard-core pornography. Many of the studies used films that are readily shown on television (especially cable television) any night of the week. And many of the movies shown today in theaters are much more explicit than those shown just a few years ago.

Social commentator Irving Kristol asked this question in a *Wall Street Journal* column: "Can anyone really believe that soft porn in our Hollywood movies, hard porn in our cable movies and violent porn in our 'rap' music is without effect? Here the average, overall impact is quite discernible to the naked eye. And at the margin, the effects, in terms most notably of illegitimacy and rape, are shockingly visible."

Christians must be careful that sexual images on television don't conform us to the world. Instead we should use discernment. Philippians 4:8 says, "Finally, brothers, whatever is true, whatever is noble, whatever is right, whatever is pure, whatever is lovely, whatever is admirable, if anything is excellent or praiseworthy, think about such things."

TV brings hitting, kicking, stabbings, shootings, and dismemberment right into homes on a daily basis.

Sex on television is at an all-time high, so we should be even more careful to screen what we and our families see. Christians should be concerned about the images we see on television.

Watching Murders Every Day

Children's greatest exposure to violence comes from television. TV shows, movies edited for television, and video games expose young children to a level of violence unimaginable just a few years ago. The American Psychological Association says the average child watches eight thousand televised murders and one hundred thousand acts of violence before finishing elementary school. That number more than doubles by the time he or she reaches age eighteen.

At a very young age, children are seeing a level of violence and mayhem that in the past may have been seen only by a few police officers and military personnel. TV brings hitting, kicking, stabbings, shootings, and dismemberment right into homes on a daily basis.

The impact on behavior is predictable. Two prominent surgeon general reports in the last two decades link violence on television and aggressive behavior in children and teenagers. In addition, the National Institute of Mental Health issued a ninety-four page report *Television and Behavior: Ten Years of Scientific Progress and Implications for the Eighties*. They found "overwhelming" scientific evidence that "excessive" violence on television spills over into the playground and the streets. In one five-year study of 732 children, "several kinds of aggression, conflicts with parents, fighting and delinquency, were all positively correlated with the total amount of television viewing."

Long-term studies are even more disturbing. University of Illinois psychologist Leonard Eron studied children at age eight and then again at eighteen. He found that television habits established at the age of eight influenced aggressive behavior throughout childhood and adolescent years. The more violent the programs preferred by boys in the third grade, the more aggressive their behavior, both at that time and ten years later. He therefore concluded that "the effect of television violence on aggression is cumulative."

Twenty years later Eron and [L.] Rowell Huesmann found the pattern continued. He and his researchers found that children who watched significant amounts of TV violence at the age of eight were consistently more likely to commit violent crimes or engage in child or spouse abuse at thirty. They concluded that "heavy exposure to televised violence is one of the causes of aggressive behavior, crime and violence in society. Television violence affects youngsters of all ages, of both genders, at all socioeconomic levels and all levels of intelligence."

Violent images on television affect children in adverse ways and Christians should be concerned about the impact.

The Biblical Perspective

Television is such a part of our lives that we often are unaware of its subtle and insidious influence. Nearly every home has a television set, so we tend to take it for granted and are often oblivious to its influence.

I've had many people tell me that they watch television, and that it has no impact at all on their worldview or behavior. However, the Bible teaches that "as a man thinks in his heart, so is he." What we view and what we think about affects our actions. And there is abundant psychological evidence that television viewing affects our worldview.

We must not ignore the growing body of data that suggests that televised imagery does affect our perceptions and behaviors.

George Gerbner and Larry Gross, working at the [University of Southern California] Annenberg School of Communications in the 1970s, found that heavy television viewers live in a scary world. "We have found that people who watch a lot of TV see the real world as more dangerous and frightening than those who watch very little. Heavy viewers are less trustful of their fellow citizens, and more fearful of the real world." Heavy viewers also tended to overestimate their likelihood of being involved in a violent crime. They defined heavy viewers as those adults who watch an average of four or more hours of television a day. Approximately one-third of all American adults fit that category.

And if this is true of adults, imagine how television violence affects children's perceptions of the world. Gerbner and Gross say, "Imagine spending six hours a day at the local movie house when you were twelve years old. No parent would have permitted it. Yet, in our sample of children, nearly half of the twelve-year-olds watch an average of six or more hours of television per day." This would mean that a large portion of young people fit into the category of heavy viewers. Their view of the world must be profoundly shaped by TV. Gerbner and Gross therefore conclude, "If adults can be so accepting of the reality of television, imagine its effect on children. By the time the average American child reaches public school, he has already spent several years in an electronic nursery school."

Television viewing affects both adults and children in subtle ways. We must not ignore the growing body of data that suggests that televised imagery does affect our perceptions and behaviors. Our worldview and our subsequent actions are affected by what we see on television. Christians, therefore, must be careful not to let television conform us to the world, but instead should develop a Christian worldview.

10

Media Violence Makes Torture Acceptable to Viewers

A.S. Hamrah

A.S. Hamrah is a writer and brand analyst and regularly publishes articles about media culture in print and online magazines.

Pictures of American prison guards torturing Iraqi prisoners mirror images from recent action movies and so-called "torture porn" films, only with reversed roles. In the movies, the perpetrators are usually third-world gangsters and fanatics and the victims are of Western origin. Movie directors teach us that torture is fun, and the photos of naked and abused prisoners in Iraq reflect that attitude. Reality and fantasy are merging into a universal attitude that to inflict pain is worth little more than a laugh.

When President [George W.] Bush sought to establish new guidelines on torture this fall [2006], he claimed that any interrogation technique that shocks the conscience would not be allowed. Hollywood filmmakers, always eager to oppose the president, go the other way in a year-end glut of torture movies that display only techniques designed to shock the conscience.

From mainstream actioners such as *Casino Royale* and *Apocalypto* to horror cut-em-ups such as *Saw III* and *Turistas* (itself a retread of 2005's breakout torture hit *Hostel*), the kind

A.S. Hamrah, "We Love to Torture," *Los Angeles Times*, December 18, 2006. Reproduced by permission of the author.

of entertainment referred to as "torture porn" combines the mise-en-scène of Abu Ghraib with screenwriting evocative of reports from Camp X-Ray.[1]

Confronting Fears

In reviewing the torture hits, critics take pains to tell readers that these movies are somehow about our collective fears of confinement and mutilation, about confronting some kind of ultimate evil that kicks us in the crotch before it cuts off our head and sends it tumbling down the stairs, punishing us for our desires.

But if we're confronting our fears, we're sure doing it exuberantly. The ingeniously imagineered punishment devices in these movies, along with their chummy torture-chamber repartee and quick recoveries from pain and abuse, aren't so much about the fear of torture as they are about the joy of it—and its necessity. Torture is a duty that filmmakers, like Tom Sawyer painting the fence, have convinced us is a lot of fun.

And like Tom, they've managed to fob the dirty work off on somebody else. In the real world of Guantánamo and secret prisons, the news is about people from other countries being tortured by people from this one. But in the movies it's the other way around.

The victims tend to be first-world dum-dums tortured by third-world thugs, as in the Brazil-set *Turistas*, in which a grab bag of English speakers from the U.S., Britain and Australia are tortured by people who speak Portuguese—except when they deliver helpful lectures in English on fair trade.

The new James Bond, we're told, is a secret agent for today, a serious time in which the stakes are high. And, like the

---

1. Abu Ghraib is the infamous prison in Iraq where prisoners were tortured and abused by American military service members. Camp X-Ray was a temporary camp at Guantánamo Bay, the controversial prison in Cuba that is run by the U.S. military and has been the focus of criticism regarding the treatment of prisoners.

kids in *Turistas*, he's tortured by a foreigner. So why does the torture in *Casino Royale* play like one of those frat pranks [conservative talk show host] Rush Limbaugh referred to when he defended Abu Ghraib guards? Reviews of *Casino Royale* shared a certain glee over the phrase "genital torture"; critics couldn't wait to titter over it. And as Bond and Le Chiffre [his opponent] trade quips about itches that need scratching, they might as well be snapping towels at each other in a locker room.

Saw III, on the other hand, functions more like a game show. It's so close to *Deal or No Deal* that Howie Mandel should play its villain, who offers his victims a chance to better themselves even as they're being tortured and killed. The message is explicit: Torture is a form of therapy that's good for its victims, who deserve—even need—it.

In the age of Abu Ghraib, the unashamed passion of torture-genre groupies is mainstream and normal.

Movie Violence and Torture Are Merging

It's only Mel Gibson, our official madman, who is held to Amnesty International standards. While the torture in *Casino Royale* is applauded as bravura, Gibson's kitschy "No Fear" version of Mayan history is described by critics as a crime against humanity. That's because for Gibson torture is deeply serious, which is not to say he's against it. While *Apocalypto* comes encoded with a message about the war in Iraq, mostly it exults in the bloodshed of sacrifice and defeat. James Wan and Leigh Whannell, the auteurs behind the *Saw* franchise, throw in phony moralizing as a kind of leavening to the carnival atmosphere of their films. But Gibson proves Samuel Johnson's aphorism that no man is a hypocrite in his pleasures. For Gibson, torture isn't the path to transcendence; it is transcendence.

In the age of Abu Ghraib, the unashamed passion of torture-genre groupies is mainstream and normal. Aintitcool. com commentator "funnyhat," writing about *See No Evil*, a torture entry from last summer [2006], is confused by anti-torture opprobrium [disgrace]. "Why does everyone call it 'torture porn'?" funnyhat asks. "It's entertainment, not a fetish! *See No Evil*, while not the greatest movie, was a great step forward for horror fans who love our torture."

"I love to torture!" Béla Lugosi shouted in a quaint (like the Geneva Convention) 1935 chiller called *The Raven*. "I tear torture from myself in torturing you," Lugosi added, showing a level of insight denied current films, whose best critic could be Limbaugh. "You ever heard of emotional release? I'm talking about people having a good time," Limbaugh said of the Abu Ghraib pranksters in 2004.

That's a definition of torture to stand next to Bush's. Here's another: Torture is what we watch acted out in front of us as we sit in movie theaters eating nachos. Torture is serial and endless, like entertainment, and comes to us in the guise of fun, as it did at Abu Ghraib. The two are beginning to merge.

11

The FCC Should Regulate Violence on Television

Christian Science Monitor

Christian Science Monitor is an international newspaper, published online Monday through Friday and in print weekly.

Because the television industry is incapable of regulating itself, the Federal Communications Commission (FCC) should take the lead in defining media violence and in taking steps to curb its corrosive effects. While free speech should not be violated and parents should not be absolved of their duty to monitor what their children watch on television, the FCC should make it easier for households to restrict violent content.

Should Congress regulate TV violence? Last month [April 2007] the Federal Communications Commission [FCC] boldly said yes. Boldly, because that position invites a strong rebuttal from defenders of free speech. And boldly again because, well, where does one draw the line on violence?

Regulation Is Needed

The FCC could have let this hornet's nest alone. But it was pushed to examine it by 39 members of the US House and has now responded with a well-reasoned report.

The television industry is not correcting itself to the satisfaction of parents—whose children watch an average of two to four hours of TV a day. Eighty-two percent of parents with young children say violence in children's programming is a major concern. Nine in 10 say it has a serious negative impact on their kids.

Government regulation is tricky here because the courts have protected violent speech and depictions under the First Amendment. But doing nothing would leave children at greater risk to models of violence. And it would leave society at greater risk of aggression committed by people who were influenced by violent media, as many studies show.

Defining violence will be a legal threading of the needle.

The arguments against government regulation can be countered:

Free speech violation. The FCC points to the precedent of regulating broadcast indecency, upheld by the Supreme Court. The court allowed restrictions because of indecency's "uniquely pervasive presence" and its accessibility to children. Indecency also ranked lower as a First Amendment right, because of its "slight social value." The parallels with violence are obvious.

Parents' main job. Yes, parents have an obligation to supervise their kids' viewing. But television violence is ubiquitous. The TV rating system and the program-blocking V-chip—tools to help parents control viewing—are "not effective," the FCC finds. To simply state that parents alone are responsible for controlling their kids' access to media violence is also to say they should be responsible for such things as safe streets.

Defining violence. The FOX drama *24* is violent, and so are cartoons, the evening news, and movie classics. Defining violence will be a legal threading of the needle. A definition must be narrowly focused on excessive or gratuitous violence to allow a broad range of contextual exceptions. Existing definitions, such as what's used for TV ratings, can serve as a starting point.

Congress Should Define and Regulate Violence

The FCC suggests that Congress define violence. That's the right place for this debate, to better reflect society's consensus and to better stand up in court. The commission also reasonably suggests that Congress restrict the hours of violent programming on broadcast TV—as is the case with indecency.

The government's right to regulate media has long been limited to the "public airwaves." That media, however, is becoming dwarfed by the Internet, satellite, cable, and microwave media. The FCC acknowledges this, at least in part, by suggesting that Congress enable cable and satellite subscribers to purchase only the channels they want rather than "bundled" channels.

Congress may resist a foray into these other media areas. But unless it acts now to claim a right to regulate in them, society might as well give up trying to have any collective controls other than consumer boycotts to curb the corrosive effects of violent media.

12

The FCC Should Not Regulate Violence on Television

Nick Gillespie

Nick Gillespie is the editor of Reason.com and Reason.tv and was the editor in chief of Reason *magazine from 2000 to 2008. He has written articles, been a commentator for many media outlets, and edited the anthology* Choice: The Best of Reason. Reason *magazine espouses libertarian values, advocating for individual liberty, free markets, and limited government.*

The notion that TV violence causes children and teenagers to act violently in school and at home is not supported by statistics and independent research. The Federal Communications Commission (FCC) is poorly equipped to do the parents' job of monitoring what children watch on television, a job that has become easier with the help of electronic aids such as the V-chip, which can block out violent or sexually explicit programs. Kid-friendly content is offered on many channels, giving parents more control than ever, yet it is not in viewers' interest to give the FCC the right to regulate what is being shown on television.

At the behest of Congress, the Federal Communications Commission [FCC] issued a report last week [April 2007] on "violent television programming and its impact on children" that calls not just for expanding governmental oversight of broadcast TV but extending content regulation to cable and satellite channels for the first time. The FCC also recommended that some shows be banned from time slots when

Nick Gillespie, "The FCC's Not Our Mommy and Daddy," *Los Angeles Times*, May 2, 2007. Reproduced by permission of the author and Reason magazine.

children might be watching and that cable and satellite operators be forced to offer "à la carte" service in which subscribers would pick and choose among individual channels.

Violent TV Is Not the Cause of Violence

Despite its sober tone, the study rests on the demonstrably false idea that violent TV breeds violence in reality, and it also fails to take seriously the vast increase in child-friendly programming and parent-empowering viewing tools. The result is a list of recommendations to Congress that seems as comically and absurdly detached from contemporary America as an episode of *SpongeBob SquarePants*.

If fantasy violence translates readily into its real-world counterpart, then why have juvenile violent crime arrests dropped steadily for 12 years?

"America is hooked on violence," laments Commissioner Jonathan S. Adelstein, who ostensibly believes that the FCC's proposed policies would make the United States safer. "Particularly in light of the spasm of unconscionable violence at Virginia Tech [when student Seung-Hui Cho killed thirty-two people and wounded many others on April 16, 2007]," he continues in his statement approving the report, "but just as importantly in light of the excessive violent crime that daily afflicts our nation, there is a basis for appropriate federal action to curb violence in the media."

Yet the report itself cites a 2001 U.S. surgeon general report that concluded "many questions remain regarding the short- and long-term effects of media violence, especially on violent behavior." More to the point, if fantasy violence translates readily into its real-world counterpart, then why have juvenile violent crime arrests dropped steadily for 12 years? According to a 2006 Department of Justice report, such arrests have fallen "to a level not seen since at least the 1970s."

The same trend is true for violent crime among the larger population. There seems little question that depictions of violence in popular culture—including TV, movies, music, video games and more—have become more frequent and more graphic since 1994. If Adelstein's thesis were true, the facts on the ground would be otherwise.

Parental Concerns Outweigh Science

But the FCC commissioners speak less as social scientists and more as parents. "I am deeply concerned about the negative effects violent programming appears to have on our children," writes Commissioner Deborah Taylor Tate. "Many of us, as parents, have witnessed our children acting out a fighting scene from an episode of *Teenage Mutant Ninja Turtles* . . . or been awakened by a frightened child climbing into bed after having a nightmare because of something they saw on television."

It's safe to say that when a quartet of do-gooder, pizza-chomping cartoon reptiles has become a predicate for federal regulation, American governance has gone seriously off the rails.

The ultimate goal of the report, she argues, is not simply to empower parents who worry about what's on TV in their house but to change "the media landscape *outside* our homes" (emphasis hers) and to increase "the amount of family-friendly, uplifting and nonviolent programming being produced."

It's safe to say that when a quartet of do-gooder, pizza-chomping cartoon reptiles has become a predicate for federal regulation, American governance has gone seriously off the rails. Similarly, if the FCC is in the business of banning children's nightmares, look for the agency to go after circus clowns any day now.

More to the point, the FCC seems to be wholly unaware that, in recent years, cable TV has become jam-packed with channels dedicated to the sort of fare Tate demands. Nickelodeon, Cartoon Network, Disney Kids, Sprout, Noggin [now Nick Jr.] and others devote most or all of their hours to kid-friendly culture.

Parental Controls Abound

At the same time, parents have gained unprecedented control over the tube. Since 2000, all new TV sets have come equipped with a government-mandated "V-chip," which allows parents to automatically block specific programs based on violence, language or sexual content ratings. The typical TV or cable/satellite box includes other controls as well that allow the blocking of channels and restrict access to the set. And, of course, all TVs come with an on/off switch. (Though as FCC Chairman Kevin J. Martin, perhaps channeling TV's laziest father, Homer Simpson, said in 2005: "You can always turn the television off and, of course, block the channels you don't want. . . . But why should you have to?") The report notes all this but assumes that the low usage rates of such tools—only about 12% of parents report regularly using the V-chip or cable channel blockers—mean that parents' wishes are being thwarted rather than fulfilled.

Maybe. But in a report that systematically misreads contemporary America, it's more likely that the FCC is simply mistaken.

13

Researchers Have Not Proven That Media Violence Merits Policy Changes

Edward Castronova

Edward Castronova is a professor of telecommunications at Indiana University. He is a founder of scholarly virtual world studies and an expert on the societies of large-scale online games. Among his academic publications on these topics are the books Synthetic Worlds: The Business and Culture of Online Games *and* Exodus to the Virtual World: How Online Fun Is Changing Reality.

The scientific research on media violence has been hampered by eagerness to prove or disprove theories on the effects of violent content on young viewers. Instead of truly trying to investigate the relationship between media and real-world aggression, researchers have only sought material supporting their hypotheses. Insufficient and misinterpreted data yield conclusions that point to a crisis that is merely stated, not proven, and give policy makers false reason to demand changes in television and media content and regulation.

There's no solid evidence that violence in media causes violence in society, certainly not at the level that would warrant any kind of policy response. Here at [the blog] Terra Nova, this has been discussed again and again. . . . Yet the issue will not die, or, more accurately, a misguided conversation

Edward Castronova, "Media Violence, Aggression, and Policy," Terra Nova Blog, May 25, 2009. www.terranova.blogs.com. Reproduced by permission of the author.

continues and at times certain points need to be reiterated. The immediate spurs to this post include a) getting an e-mail about video game violence effects from an undergraduate at another school, b) seeing one of Indiana's PhD students give a talk on video game violence, and c) seeing media effects being debated at the International Communications Association meeting in Chicago this past weekend [May 2009]. Researchers continue to pursue evidence for a causal link between violence in media and real-world violence, and important people in the real world still think there's some sort of emergency.

Media Violence Research Has Produced No Results

Common-sense objections to the agenda and the urgency are legion. . . . Yet there are deeper issues, of a scholarly nature, that need to be addressed as well. Research in the field of media violence effects is generally ill-conceived, poorly executed, and result-driven. I have seen few things that I would describe as findings—results that become a permanent part of my view of the world and how it works. Before any more PhD students waste their careers on bad science, let's once again put the cards on the table.

To begin at the end: Scientific research should not be framed as the pursuit of evidence for something. To do so violates the important norm of disinterestedness. You are not supposed to care how the numbers turn out. The proper way to think of things is "What causes Y?" not "Can I find evidence that X might affect Y?" The Y here is violence in society. We know that the main causes of violence in society are parents and peers. A disinterested scholar would stop there. Yet in media violence research, the norm is to go looking for a link. One senses that in most papers nothing would be sent to the journal until some evidence for the link was found.

How does one get that sense? This is the second major issue: significance. In scholarly writing, the term significance refers to a very specialized statistical feature known in most fields as statistical significance. It is a measure of the accuracy of a finding. It is also widely misunderstood and improperly applied. (How do I know? Training under econometrician Arthur Goldberger.) Look at it this way: You are the captain of the ship. The engineer comes and says that some rivets in the hull are weakening and are about to pop. Yet you can only fix them one at a time. Your first question is, what rivet is weakest? That is where the engineer should start. Oddly, in psychology and the social sciences, one insists that the engineer start working instead on the rivet whose weakness is most accurately measured. "We think rivet 12 is weakest, but we know more about rivet 34, so let's start there. By the way, rivet 34 seems to be pretty strong."

The media violence field gets its energy from its ostensible policy relevance.

Social Sciences Fail the Public

In media violence research, it appears to be a universal practice that the accuracy of an effect's measurement is presented always first, and often exclusively. The size of the effect is considered secondary, if it is considered at all. In my experience of articles and presentations in this field, I have yet to see a sentence in the following form: "All else equal, a 10 percent increase in this measure of media violence leads to an X% increase in this measure of social violence." This is a very simple simulation of effect, and it seems never to be done.

Here's how the first two issues are related: If the research paradigm is to hunt for effects, and the standard of a "finding" is based on statistical significance, it is usually easy to produce the desired result. The nature of statistical significance is such that if you mess around with the data set enough, eventually some set of controls and procedures causes the computer to pop out an asterisk indicating statistical significance on the media violence variable. This is why the paper says, "Although no overall media-aggression link was found, a link was found among children who identify with a violent character." Meaning, if you split the data into those-who-identify and those-who-don't, you find the desired link in the former group. In any reasonably complex data set, there will be some subgroup or some tweak that generates statistical significance. It's a mechanical thing in the end. And thus, when a researcher produces an entire career of papers showing the same result over and over, you get the sense that the disinterestedness norm is being violated. This scholar is not in the least disinterested. He knows what he is after and he is going to find it. The only way that disinterestedness could be restored in this field would be for scholars to forget about statistical significance and examine instead the real-world significance of findings, by means of these simple simulation sentences. Let's talk about the rivets that seem weakest. Assertions of real-world significance are not popped out by SPSS [a computer program used for statistical analysis]. They cannot be cooked. If media effects researchers want to be trusted, they should abandon statistical significance as the measure of truth.

You could, if you wanted, study the relationship of dogs' ears to the sounds of motors, but you'll never find solid evidence that dogs get happy when their people drive into the garage.

Asking the Wrong Questions

The issue of significance goes beyond statistical significance, however, into the realm of policy significance. The media violence field gets its energy from its ostensible policy relevance. Yet the research questions are not framed in a way that is helpful for policy. The policy question is simple: If we regulate media violence, will social violence fall? But the research asks: If we expose this person to violent media, how will he act in the next hour? The latter is not relevant to the former. Or, there does not seem to be a good theory explaining why the latter is relevant. Yes, there are diagrams of boxes and arrows known as theories, but they are really just conceptual overviews, informal and heuristic [educated guesses], and cannot be used to measure or explain how a social effect emerges from a lab effect. As an example, suppose we use an Aggressometer to measure a person's aggressive mental state, and find that viewing *Star Wars* increases the Aggressometer by 20 percent. The question now becomes, if we show *Star Wars* generally in the public, we are generally going to have a 20 percent increase in Aggressometer readings. What theory tells me how this is specifically going to change the crime rate? I need to know that, because I need to evaluate policy in a common-sense way. Keeping a million kids from watching *Star Wars* costs society $7m [million] in lost entertainment value. Is the purported value of crime reduction more or less than that? A box-and-arrow diagram does not help. If the research is going to stay focused on the mind, we need a good theory to connect mind outcomes to policy outcomes—otherwise the research isn't relevant for policy and should be labeled as such: "Warning: Not for Use by Legislators." . . .

Why is it so hard to find answers in this area? Fuzziness. The media violence–aggression field has chosen to study two things that do not admit accurate observation. What is media violence? What kind of a thing is it? The policy debate seems to assume it is a continuous variable that acts as a gloss on a piece of media. Thus, you can apparently make a movie less violent by taking away an explosion. Similarly, what is aggression? It appears to be taken as some sort of negative gloss on a person, such that if you make them more aggressive you make the world a worse place. Needless to say, taking aggression and violence as separable from the whole entities in which they are observed is a fuzzy and probably fundamentally wrongheaded way to approach things. You could, if you wanted, study the relationship of dogs' ears to the sounds of motors, but you'll never find solid evidence that dogs get happy when their people drive into the garage. You need to study dogs and people, not ears and motors. In fact the only reason you might study ears and motors separately is that you had some agenda to promote the motor industry by showing that it makes dogs happy. But of course, that wouldn't be disinterested.

Going in the Wrong Direction

I cooked up a silly example. Consider the following report:

> Textiles scholars have studied the effect of softness in cloth on affection. Children rubbed with soft cloth as opposed to scratchy cloth self-report significantly higher levels of affection and exhibit more affectionate behaviors (hugging teddy bears, for example). Responding to these findings, and acting out of a concern about the dramatic declines in affection in recent decades, the American Academy of Pediatrics recommends that children's exposure to soft cloth be maximized. The State of California has mandated that all cloth sold to minors must meet a minimum standard of SS+ (from the industry's cloth softness self-rating system). Unfortunately, the laws have been struck down as an improper extension of government authority, as stated in the 28th Amendment ("Congress shall make no law abridging the freedom of the textile manufacturer"). Nonetheless, pressure continues for some sort of government response to the softness-affection crisis.

Ridiculous, of course. The PTA's insistence that school kids wear velvet boots would last one rainy day, and that would be it. But to be more specific about what's wrong here:

1. The research deals with vague value-laden concepts, not objective observables.

2. The findings are not disinterested. Somebody's looking for something.

3. There is no evidence of a crisis at the social level.

4. The pediatricians' recommendation to parents assumes thoroughly incompetent parents.

5. So does the policy.

6. The policy asserts an unrealistic level of measurement and control.

7. The relevance of the findings for the policy is nowhere demonstrated.

8. "Significantly" refers to statistical significance, not real-world significance.

There's not much difference between the cloth-softness debate and the media violence debate, unfortunately.

People and their art are certainly worthy of study. But if we are going to be scientific about it, there are certain rules that must be followed. Following those rules might mean that some questions simply elude us. . . .

In the end, I suspect that media violence research has been motivated primarily by aesthetic concerns.

Questioning the Motivations of Media Violence Research

If you want me to believe that regulating violence in media would make our world a better place, you'll have to walk me around the world and through history, and help me to imaginatively experience a culture in which control of expression led to more happiness. I wander around in history a lot—it's been a hobby for decades—and I don't know of any such culture. Even fantasizing about the future, I am not seeing anything good.

In the end, I suspect that media violence research has been motivated primarily by aesthetic concerns. *The Three Stooges* is disgusting and vulgar, whereas *King Lear* is sublime. Why are we watching so much crap? Back in the day, you could make the aesthetic plea directly: Look here, you are watching bad art, and you shouldn't—just because it is bad. Today, aesthetic disgust gets channeled into sciency-sounding condemnations of entire media forms for their "effects." In our free-thinking age, no one can effectively change anyone's mind by asserting that *Grand Theft Auto* is simply adolescent, an 1812 Overture of bullying and nastiness, of low appeal. But because the age is also utilitarian, you can make the case that *Grand Theft Auto* has "bad effects": like cigarettes, you say, its use harms others.

Organizations to Contact

The editors have compiled the following list of organizations concerned with the issues debated in this book. The descriptions are derived from materials provided by the organizations. All have publications or information available for interested readers. The list was compiled on the date of publication of the present volume; names, addresses, phone and fax numbers, and e-mail and Internet addresses may change. Be aware that many organizations take several weeks or longer to respond to inquiries, so allow as much time as possible.

American Civil Liberties Union (ACLU)
125 Broad Street, 18th Floor, New York, NY   10004
(212) 549-2500 • fax: (212) 549-2650
Web site: www.aclu.org

The American Civil Liberties Union (ACLU) is an organization that works to defend the rights and principles delineated in the Declaration of Independence and the U.S. Constitution. It opposes the censorship of any form of speech, including media depictions of violence. The ACLU publishes the semi-annual *Civil Liberties*, policy statements, and reports.

American Psychological Association (APA)
750 First Street NE, Washington, DC   20002-4242
(800) 374-2721 • fax: (202) 336-5502
e-mail: psycinfo@apa.org
Web site: www.apa.org

The American Psychological Association (APA) is the world's largest organization of psychologists. Although the APA opposes censorship, it asserts that viewing television can have potential dangers for children. It publishes numerous books, journals, and videos, and provides information online, such as "Strategies to Reduce the Impact of Media Violence in Young Children's Lives."

Cato Institute

1000 Massachusetts Avenue NW, Washington, DC 20001
(202) 842-0200 • fax: (202) 842-3490
Web site: www.cato.org

The Cato Institute is a libertarian public policy research foundation. It evaluates government policies and offers reform proposals and commentary on its Web site. Its publications include the Cato Policy Analysis series of reports, the magazine *Regulation*, the *Cato Policy Report*, numerous studies, and the article "Rating Entertainment Ratings: How Well Are They Working for Parents, and What Can Be Done to Improve Them?"

Center for Media Literacy (CML)

23852 Pacific Coast Highway, Suite 472, Malibu, CA 90265
(310) 456-1225 • fax: (310) 456-0020
e-mail: cml@medialit.org
Web site: www.medialit.org

Center for Media Literacy (CML) is an organization providing public education and professional development. CML works nationally to help young people develop critical thinking and media production skills. Its books can be purchased online, and its Web site offers free background information and articles about research in media violence.

Dove Foundation

535 East Fulton, Suite 1A, Grand Rapids, MI 49503
(616) 454-5021 • fax: (616) 454-5036
e-mail: movies@dove.org
Web site: www.dove.org

The Dove Foundation promotes family friendly entertainment based on Judeo-Christian values free from the pressure of commercial interests. The organization believes in a positive approach of commending high-quality, wholesome movies rather than condemning filmmakers for not meeting those standards. It provides reviews of movies and entertainment news online.

The International Clearinghouse on Children, Youth and Media

Nordicom, University of Gothenburg, Box 713
Göteborg SE 405 30
  Sweden
46 31 786 1000 • fax: 46 31 786 4655
e-mail: clearinghouse@nordicom.gu.se
Web site: www.nordicom.gu.se

The aim of the International Clearinghouse on Children, Youth and Media is to increase awareness and knowledge about children, youth, and media by providing a basis for relevant policy making, contributing to public debate, and enhancing children's and young people's media literacy. It aims to inform researchers, policy makers, media professionals, voluntary organizations, teachers, students, and other interested individuals. Books on media violence can be purchased on its Web site.

Media Coalition

275 Seventh Avenue, Suite 1504, New York, NY   10001
(212) 587-4025 • fax: (212) 587-2436
Web site: www.mediacoalition.org

The Media Coalition is a trade association defending the First Amendment rights of publishers, booksellers, librarians, motion picture and video game producers, and consumers in the United States. It opposes restrictions to violent content and reports news on current lawsuits and developments in the entertainment industry on its Web site. Media Coalition also publishes the report *Shooting the Messenger: Why Censorship Won't Stop Violence.*

National Center for Children Exposed to Violence (NCCEV)

Yale University, Child Study Center, 230 South Frontage Road
New Haven, CT   06520-7900
(877) 49 NCCEV (496-2238) • fax: (203) 785-4608
e-mail: colleen.vadala@yale.edu
Web site: www.nccev.org

The National Center for Children Exposed to Violence (NCCEV) works to increase the capacity of individuals and communities to reduce the incidence and impact of violence on children and families. It trains and supports the professionals who provide intervention and treatment to children and families affected, and seeks to increase public awareness of the effects of violence—including media violence—on children, families, communities, and society. Brochures and bibliographies are available online or can be purchased.

Teachers Resisting Unhealthy Children's Entertainment (TRUCE)
PO Box 441261, Somerville, MA   02144
e-mail: truce@truceteachers.org
Web site: www.truceteachers.org

Teachers Resisting Unhealthy Children's Entertainment (TRUCE) is a national group of educators concerned about how children's entertainment is affecting the play and behavior of children in classrooms nationwide. Its goals are to raise public awareness about the negative effects of the violent and stereotyped media and to support parents' and teachers' efforts to deal with these issues regarding the media. TRUCE offers guides and resources online.

Bibliography

Books

Craig A. Anderson, Douglas A. Gentile, and Katherine E. Buckley
Violent Video Game Effects on Children and Adolescents: Theory, Research, and Public Policy. New York: Oxford University Press, 2007.

Mark Andrejevic
Reality TV: The Work of Being Watched. Lanham, MD: Rowman & Littlefield Publishers, 2004.

Hector Avalos
Fighting Words: The Origins of Religious Violence. Amherst, NY: Prometheus Books, 2005.

Martin Barker and Julian Petley, eds.
Ill Effects: The Media/Violence Debate. London: Routledge, 2001.

Jonathan Bignell
Big Brother: Reality TV in the Twenty-First Century. New York: Palgrave Macmillan, 2005.

Anita Biressi and Heather Nunn
Reality TV: Realism and Revelation. London: Wallflower, 2005.

Jane Buckingham, ed.
What's Next: The Experts' Guide: Predictions from 50 of America's Most Compelling People. New York: HarperCollins, 2008.

Canadian Teachers' Federation | *Kids' Take on Media: What 5,700 Canadian Kids Say About TV, Movies, Video and Computer Games and More.* Ottawa, Ontario, Canada: Canadian Teachers' Federation, 2003.

Nancy E. Dowd, Dorothy G. Singer, and Robin Fretwell Wilson, eds. | *Handbook of Children, Culture, and Violence.* Thousand Oaks, CA: Sage Publications, 2006.

Jonathan L. Freedman | *Media Violence and Its Effect on Aggression: Assessing the Scientific Evidence.* Toronto, Ontario, Canada: University of Toronto Press, 2002.

Douglas A. Gentile, ed. | *Media Violence and Children: A Complete Guide for Parents and Professionals.* Westport, CT: Praeger, 2003.

Interactive Digital Software Association | *Video Games and Youth Violence: Examining the Facts.* Washington, DC: Interactive Digital Software Association, 2001.

Henry Jenkins | *Convergence Culture: Where Old and New Media Collide.* New York: New York University Press, 2006.

Deborah Jermyn | *Crime Watching: Investigating Real Crime TV.* London: I.B. Tauris & Co., 2007.

Gerard Jones   *Killing Monsters: Why Children Need Fantasy, Super Heroes, and Make-Believe Violence*. New York: Basic Books, 2002.

Misha Kavka   *Reality Television, Affect and Intimacy: Reality Matters*. New York: Palgrave Macmillan, 2008.

Steven J. Kirsh   *Children, Adolescents, and Media Violence: A Critical Look at the Research*. Thousand Oaks, CA: Sage Publications, 2006.

Arthur G. Miller, ed.   *The Social Psychology of Good and Evil*. New York: Guilford Press, 2004.

Jolyon Mitchell   *Media Violence and Christian Ethics*. Cambridge, UK: Cambridge University Press, 2007.

Susan Murray and Laurie Ouellette, eds.   *Reality TV: Remaking Television Culture*. 2nd ed. New York: New York University Press, 2009.

W. James Potter   *The 11 Myths of Media Violence*. Thousand Oaks, CA: Sage Publications, 2003.

Harold Schechter   *Savage Pastimes: A Cultural History of Violent Entertainment*. New York: St. Martin's Press, 2005.

Karen Sternheimer   *It's Not the Media: The Truth About Pop Culture's Influence on Children*. Boulder, CO: Westview Press, 2003.

James P. Steyer   *The Other Parent: The Inside Story of the Media's Effect on Our Children.* New York: Atria Books, 2002.

David Trend   *The Myth of Media Violence: A Critical Introduction.* Malden, MA: Blackwell Publishing, 2007.

Bryan Vossekuil,   *The Final Report and Findings of the Safe School Initiative: Implications for the Prevention of School Attacks in the United States.* Washington, DC: United States Secret Service and United States Department of Education, 2002.
Robert A. Fein,
Marisa Reddy,
Randy Borum,
and William
Modzeleski

Periodicals

American   "Media Violence: Committee on Public Education," *Pediatrics,* vol. 108, no. 5, November 2001.
Academy of
Pediatrics

Craig A.   "The Influence of Media Violence on Youth," *Psychological Science in the Public Interest,* vol. 4, no. 3, December 2003.
Anderson et al.

Asian News   "Violent Media 'Indeed Impacts Adolescent Behaviour,'" November 20, 2008.
International

Birmingham Post   "Why We Must Protect Our Children from Violent Films," September 27, 2007.
(England)

Brad J. Bushman and Craig A. Anderson
"Media Violence and the American Public: Scientific Facts Versus Media Misinformation," *American Psychologist*, vol. 56, no. 6/7, June/July 2001.

Brad J. Bushman and Joanne Cantor
"Media Ratings for Violence and Sex: Implications for Policymakers and Parents," *American Psychologist*, vol. 58, no. 2, February 2003.

Joanne Cantor and Barbara J. Wilson
"Media and Violence: Intervention Strategies for Reducing Aggression," *Media Psychology*, vol. 5, no. 4, November 2003.

Jason L. Deselms and Joanne D. Altman
"Immediate and Prolonged Effects of Videogame Violence," *Journal of Applied Social Psychology*, vol. 33, no. 8, August 2003.

Jeanne B. Funk et al.
"Violence Exposure in Real-Life, Video Games, Television, Movies, and the Internet: Is There Desensitization?" *Journal of Adolescence*, February 2004.

Douglas A. Gentile and J. Ronald Gentile
"Violent Video Games as Exemplary Teachers: A Conceptual Analysis," *Journal of Youth and Adolescence*, vol. 37, no. 2, February 2008.

Douglas A. Gentile, Muniba Saleem, and Craig A. Anderson
"Public Policy and the Effects of Media Violence on Children," *Social Issues and Policy Review*, 2007.

Gary W. Giumetti and Patrick M. Markey — "Violent Video Games and Anger as Predictors of Aggression," *Journal of Research in Personality*, 2007.

Peter S. Goodman — "Violent Media May Trim Real Violence, Study Says," *International Herald Tribune*, January 8, 2008.

Kevin Haninger and Kimberly M. Thompson — "Content and Ratings of Teen-Rated Video Games," *Journal of the American Medical Association*, February 2004.

Alice Holbrook and Amy E. Singer — "When Bad Girls Go Good: Models of the Self and Reality on VH1's *Flavor of Love Girls: Charm School*," *Journal of Popular Film & Television*, Spring 2009.

David Kushner — "With a Nudge or Vibration, Game Reality Reverberates," *New York Times*, July 3, 2003.

Monique A. Levermore and Gina L. Salisbury — "The Relationship Between Virtual & Actual Aggression: Youth Exposure to Violent Media," *Forensic Examiner*, June 22, 2009.

Michel Marriott — "Making High-Tech Play Less Work," *New York Times*, February 12, 2004.

Andrew K. Przybylski, Richard M. Ryan, and C. Scott Rigby — "The Motivating Role of Violence in Video Games," *Personality and Social Psychology Bulletin*, vol. 35, no. 2, 2009.

Jill Richmond and J. Clare Wilson	"Are Graphic Media Violence, Aggression and Moral Disengagement Related?" *Psychiatry, Psychology and Law*, July 1, 2008.
Victoria Rideout and Elizabeth Hamel	"The Media Family: Electronic Media in the Lives of Infants, Toddlers, Preschoolers and Their Parents," Henry J. Kaiser Family Foundation, May 2006. www.kff.org.
Lawrence I. Rosenkoetter et al.	"Mitigating the Harmful Effects of Violent Television," *Journal of Applied Developmental Psychology*, vol. 25, no. 1., January–February 2004.
Kaveri Subrahmanyam	"Youth and Media: Opportunities for Development or Lurking Dangers? Children, Adolescents, and the Media," *Journal of Applied Developmental Psychology*, August 2003.

Index